The Collective
Memory

The Collective Memory

MAURICE HALBWACHS

Translated from the French
by Francis J. Ditter, Jr.
and Vida Yazdi Ditter

HARPER COLOPHON BOOKS
HARPER & ROW, PUBLISHERS
NEW YORK, CAMBRIDGE, HAGERSTOWN, PHILADELPHIA,
SAN FRANCISCO, LONDON, MEXICO CITY, SÃO PAULO, SYDNEY

This work was first published in French under the title *La Mémoire collective*. Copyright 1950 Presses Universitaires de France.

THE COLLECTIVE MEMORY. English translation copyright © 1980 by Harper & Row, Publishers, Inc. Introduction copyright © 1980 by Mary Douglas. All rights reserved. Printed in the United States of America. No part of this book may be used or reproduced in any manner whatsoever without written permission except in the case of brief quotations embodied in critical articles and reviews. For information address Harper & Row, Publishers, Inc., 10 East 53rd Street, New York, N.Y. 10022. Published simultaneously in Canada by Fitzhenry & Whiteside Limited, Toronto.

FIRST EDITION

Designed by Robin Malkin

Library of Congress Cataloging in Publication Data

Halbwachs, Maurice, 1877–1945.
   The collective memory.

   (Harper colphon books; CN/800)
   Translation of La mémoire collective.
   Includes index.
   1. Memory. 2. Social psychology. I. Title.
HM267.H313   302   74–18576
ISBN 0-06-090800-9 (pbk.)

80 81 82 83 84 10 9 8 7 6 5 4 3 2 1

Contents

Introduction: Maurice Halbwachs (1877-1945)

Maurice Halbwachs' publications are diverse. They include statistical treatises, social criticism, reviews of the social sciences, and several major works on consciousness. Though the themes are various, they are not scattered or irrelevant to a central program—the analysis of the process of memory. This topic he acquired direct from Henri Bergson, his first master. As a pupil at the Lycée Henri IV, dazzled by Bergson's intellectual power, he was won by his teacher to seek a vocation in philosophy. As is well known, Bergson's whole metaphysical scheme pivoted upon a particular conception of time. He would deplore his fellow philosophers' undue concentration upon space, arguing that time was neglected and misrepresented by the practice of measuring its passage only by changes in space: the spatial reference obscures the essential subjective experience. When Halbwachs' own approach was formulated it opposed nearly everything that Bergson taught, courteously but uncompromisingly.

For a pupil to have stayed with Bergsonian principles would have opened certain intellectual opportunities. For example, the phenomenologists Husserl and Schutz worked within an intuitionist theory of knowledge justified by Bergson and they counted him among their lineage ancestors. That Halbwachs did not choose this path may perhaps be explained by the counterattraction of the other intellectual enterprises to which he eventually subscribed. Halbwachs was competent in mathematical statistics and concerned with contemporary social problems. At the turn of the century the social sciences were offering exciting prospects of new understanding. But they were aligned under the wrong banners for a loyal Bergsonian scholar.

Bergson was an independent thinker, an innovator in European philosophy, or rather he dared to go back to an earlier philosophy of innate ideas which stood discredited in post-Kantian traditions of enquiry. Taking no notice at all of the current criticisms of intuitions, he announced his own account of knowledge comprising two kinds of thinking, one based on logical reasoning, the other based on direct intuitions which cannot be described or analyzed, only intuited subjectively.[1] On this basis he put time as the central problem of philosophy; for him a direct, subjective perception of inner time is the source of knowledge about the self and an assurance of free will. He contrasted the richness and self-evident truth of this intuition with the pitfalls, plodding, and false analogies of logical comparison and mathematical measurement.[2] His subjectivist philosophy allowed him confidently to assert beliefs which troubled philosophers deep in epistemological criticism. In an age when many thinkers were struggling with what they called the body-mind problem,[3] he provided his own optimistic solution, which was in favor of mind and the autonomy of spiritual values and against deterministic, mechanistic conceptions of human behavior.

One of the troubles with intuitionist theories is that if, after self-inspection, one is not seized by the alleged clear and immediate intuition, there is no further scope for conversation. No analysis or new reasoning can convince another of the matter at issue: either you recognize the intuition or you don't. Presumably the young

[1] "Essai sur les données immédiates de la conscience," Paris, 1889.
[2] See his criticism of Einstein's theory of relativity, "Durée et Simultanéité: à propos de la théorie d'Einstein," Paris, 1922.
[3] "Matière et mémoire: essai sur la relation du corps à l'esprit," Paris, 1896. "L'Ame et le corps," lecture published in *La Materialisme actuel*, Paris, 1916.

Halbwachs began to have doubts. He might well have found the necessary intellectual loyalties too constraining. Bergson was the declared enemy of materialism, empiricism, and determinism. This ruled out of court any joining in new explorations in psychology and sociology or other intellectual ventures aligned, however indirectly, with Marxist views or the positivist methods of Auguste Comte. The materialists and empiricists—so-called because of their commitments to objectivity and therefore to measurement—were not against but rather drew inspiration from physical science, but Bergson denounced their limitations in matters of human psychology. A further attraction for a young man with a social conscience would be the implicit alliance of the nascent social sciences with critics of social injustice. Bergson was, of course, also against injustice and in favor of human freedom, but his spiritual emphasis implied that empirical inquiries, pursued with inevitably too crude measuring rods, were doomed to miss the quintessential truths about man. He did not go so far as to say that such inquiries were an unnecessary (if not a misguided) waste of time, but they did not figure on his agenda of urgent intellectual tasks. To share his master's loyalties, Halbwachs would have had to remain a pure metaphysician. From these beginnings he disengaged himself in two steps.

First, he went to Hanover to study the works of Leibnitz. It is not clear whether Bergson blessed this journey. He might even have proposed it for his pupil. He often used to contrast his own philosophical position with that of Descartes, his greatest French predecessor. Over and over again he would criticize Descartes for leading Western thought down a mistaken path, paying undue honor to knowledge acquired from the measurable qualities of things, to mathematics as the source of truth. In particular, Descartes' focus on geometrization as a method of approaching reality resulted, so Bergson argued, in blocking our possibilities of appreciating the experience of time, since time is only measured by changes in space. Leibnitz was a near-contemporary critic of Descartes. For anyone who rejected the English empiricist line of criticism and who sought other non-Cartesian options in philosophy, a return to Leibnitz was a reasonable strategy. This towering seventeenth-century figure had taken an attractive middle line in controversies of his time. Moreover, from Bergson's point of view he was doctrinally sound on spiritual autonomy, freedom, and the immortality of the soul. Halbwachs' new master, for such Leibnitz became, was a brilliant mathematician who had challenged the great Newton with his claim to be the first to invent differential calculus. Halbwachs worked on Leibnitz's unpublished papers and helped to catalogue them. He was nominated to be one of the editors of an international edition of Leibnitz's works, a scheme put off by the outbreak of World War I. Leibnitz is frequently quoted by Halbwachs in many unexpectedly apt places. His little textbook on the philosopher, published in 1907, described in admirably simple style what he found important in Leibnitz.

First, he emphasized Leibnitz's attack on intuition. Next, he quoted his recommendations on behalf of logic and mathematics as the superior forms of knowledge. Third, he detailed his model of differential calculus for developing a little-by-little, gradualist approach to philosophical controversies. According to Leibnitz, most discontinuities in thought are artificial and misleading. Tracing minute changes over many strands is a way of dismantling the formidable old boundaries of philosophical dispute; even the intractable problem of mind versus matter takes on a milder aspect when the hard dichotomies are gradually dissolved.

Between clear and obscure, there are little transitions.[4]

An intuition is a calculation without signs. It does not belong to our nature, which is able to proceed by continuous movement from cruder to finer symbolising.[5]

The mind is not a *tabula rasa*, empty of experience, nor does it start with innate ideas awakened by experience. The Cartesians and the empiricists both fail to take gradual changes into account. Innate ideas are neither all ready-made, nor pure potential.[6]

[4] *Leibniz*, p. 72.
[5] Ibid., p. 79.
[6] Ibid., p. 68.

According to Bergson, forgetting is due to obstacles, remembering is a removal of obstacles. Later Halbwachs would argue that forgetting is due to vague and piecemeal impressions and remembering a process of fitting them together under suitable stimuli. Bergson's view supposed that the whole of past experience is always present to us, like the printed pages of a book, complete and entire in subterranean galleries of the mind. Leibnitz, according to Halbwachs, held a very similar view:

> Our present thought is not only heavy with thoughts to come—all thoughts and all impressions leave their trace in us in the form of conscious memories and indistinct recollections. . . . Our perceptions lose their clarity; but they remain active and thanks to them we have the notion of our own identity. Nothing is forgotten; once attention is renewed these little perceptions become clear once more, and so we remember.[7]

Halbwachs' own formula played up the indistinctness and incompleteness of past recollections and attributed the ability to remember to partial renewal of the old experiences by means of external stimuli, such as seeing a friend or revisiting a scene. We remember when some new reminder helps us to piece together small, scattered, and indistinct bits of the past.

Bergson needed his concept of the unity and completeness of past experience stored up in the unconscious: it was part of his theory of the intuition of personal identity. So Halbwachs' insistence on indistinct and partial memories undermines his first teacher's theories more critically than would appear out of context.

One can recognize a charter for Halbwachs' future non-Bergsonian work from the following, which he attributed to Leibnitz:

> Individual consciousness is not the only way in which personal identity is constituted: contacts with other people and with other things can supplement it.[8]

After this, Halbwachs relegated the body-mind problem to a lower status than Bergson claimed for it. He probably expected to have

[7] Ibid., p. 71.
[8] Ibid., p. 80.

no more worries about differences of degree and differences of kind, differences of quantity and differences of quality, intuition and intelligence, inner-time and outer-time. By immersing himself deeply in the dead metaphysician's thought he emancipated himself from the living one, and absolved himself from having to do metaphysics on his own account.

After the sojourn in Hanover, Halbwachs called upon Emile Durkheim in Paris. He claimed to have finished with philosophy and asked to be trained as a sociologist. One might suppose from the sequel that he then stopped concerning himself with such philosophical problems as the experience of time. But Durkheim himself was a proponent of an alternative view of the subject. In choosing Durkheim, rather than another sociologist, Halbwachs was decidedly going over to the enemy. He was not leaving Bergson's territory in any neutral sense, but rather was moving into a good position from which to prepare an attack on it. For Durkheim and Mauss (his nephew and colleague) had consistently developed conceptions of time which did not in any way rest upon the discoveries of individual psychology; they presented time not as an intuition, but as a social construct. However, it was a long while before Halbwachs addressed the subject. He turned first to contemporary social problems.

In 1908 he wrote an article criticizing municipal authorities for not providing public parks for the use of workers. The argument is couched in terms of surplus value created by the workers but not accruing to them, is avowedly socialist, quotes Fourier, and relays to French policy makers the news of experiments in town planning legislation and progressive taxation in Germany and Great Britain. A 1909 study describes the urban dislocation caused by private enterprise in the development of Paris during the previous century. The account is supported by a statistical analysis of changes in the value of land, i.e., the unequal rates of compensation allowed for dispossessing the rich as contrasted with the poor landowners. Had he continued his work in direct economic and political analysis, a field that was becoming more and more professional and effective in his lifetime, he would surely have made his mark. The influence of

Durkheim, however, drew him toward abstract philosophical issues. He published two lengthy papers on social statistics criticizing utilitarian philosophy, in particular its starting point from individual psychology: his dissertation on working-class living standards in 1913 and *Les Origines du sentiment religieux d'après Durkheim* in 1924. These are both extensions to modern life of Durkheim's philosophy. Not until all this was accomplished did he return in 1925, at the age of 48, to memory and time in *Les Cadres sociaux de la mémoire* (1925). Before discussing this, our central topic, it is helpful to say a little more about his third teacher, Durkheim, with whom Halbwachs was associated as a student and collaborator in *L'Année Sociologique* until Durkheim's death in 1917.

Durkheim was another stern founder of a school of thought who, like Bergson, brooked no disagreement among his followers. One might say that Durkheim was a sociologist first and foremost. He became, as it were, a philosopher by necessity, since his central concern was to uncover the sources of social solidarity through a theory of collective consciousness. In Halbwachs' work, Bergson and Durkheim are confronted: the former, individualistic, psychologistic, subjectivist; the latter, collectivist, sociological (indeed rather outspoken against psychology doing duty for sociological explanation), and seeking objectivity in the tradition of Comte's positivism. In spite of these contrasts, there is a curious parallel in their choice of fundamental theoretical issues. In post-Kantian philosophy the major initiatives had been taken by Hegel and Marx. To carry on a dialogue across the Franco-German border after 1870 was perhaps less congenial than before, and certainly the flow of international communications in psychology and philosophy that was still quite strong at the turn of the century gradually diminished until 1914, when it almost stopped. One senses an increasing need to prove the value of French culture, its uniqueness and independence. Both Bergson and Durkheim wrote as if developments since Kant need not count. Neither was interested in empiricist criticism in the theory of knowledge. Both tried to improve upon Kant's work. They took him up at the fundamental level of his criticism of innate ideas and his theory that there are two necessary categories of understanding, time and space, and that these categories are definitely not intuitions, ideas, or modes of reasoning, but conditions of thought. Both scholars offered large, system-building alternatives. Bergson started by separating the experience of time from that of space, insisting that the former had never been studied apart from its spatial measurements. He identified inner time (not the external time which is susceptible to objective measurement) as a direct and immediate intuition of the mind. This approach explained and justified the sense of personal identity and asserted the dominance of pure thought over physiological processes in the brain. Durkheim proposed not two but three necessary conditions for human understanding, adding the social condition to the categories of time and space. It is as if they had both looked at Kant's achievement and decided that the best place to enter the argument would be to say something more about those fundamental Kantian categories of understanding.

For Durkheim the prospect of individual thought is impossible to contemplate, almost an absurdity, since language and categorization arise together in social intercourse. The source of morality and religion is the individual's experience of society as a moral force greater than himself, and requiring his allegiance. From time to time moral sentiments are fanned into strong emotions by ceremonies of intense social interaction, times of religious effervescence, when the moral authority of society is easily assimilated to the idea of God. To understand the social factors sustaining individual consciousness was his central program of research.

Two questions in this program were to be taken up by Halbwachs, the totally convinced disciple. One was how moral and religious fervor remain alive between the moments of effervescence. In the quest for an answer, Durkheim emphasized the physical props and spatial mappings that sustain cognition. But this kind of answer only forced the question about religion to be formulated more sharply: If most categories of thought can be held in the mind because of the possibility of pointing to the physical object of reference, do not religious categories have special difficulty in remaining stable since they have no physical reference but only refer to society itself, an abstract idea in the minds of those who live together? To answer this, Durkheim developed his theory of totemism and other religious beliefs that require physical representations of abstract ideas. He also argued, following Comte, that spatial categories have a natural stability that makes them capable of sustaining the evanescent moods of social consciousness.

Of the second generation of Durkheim's colleagues, Halbwachs was particularly interested in modern industrial society and capable of drawing his examples from it. His early training in metaphysics made him subtle; his interest in social criticism and his statistical bent gave him a specific role to play.

Here I should mention briefly the studies which are specifically sociological, less concerned with philosophy, before introducing his other works on memory and this volume, *The Collective Memory*.

In *La Classe ouvrière et les niveaux de vie* (1913), Halbwachs used two important sets of German statistics, collected in 1909, to analyze workers' expenditures and to propose a sociological theory of needs. A characteristic expenditure pattern among workers was already established and known as Engel's law, according to which the lower paid spend a larger proportion of their income on food than other income groups, an expenditure pattern which is typically not responsive to small changes in income. The kind of easy theorizing that has accompanied this observation, then and since, tends to explain it by reference to the bedrock necessities of survival which supposedly control the lower-paid worker's expenditures. We still find economists subscribing to physiological theories of needs. Halbwachs counterproposed that perception of needs is determined by social class. He used Durkheim's theory of collective representations to give a sociological definition of class and a sociological approach to consumption. Goods are used for establishing social relations. Hence the worker, by reason of his isolated and powerless position in society, has no call for unlimited expenditures on housing, travel, or other things. He can relate to only two social groupings, his family and the public life of the streets—the first with food, the second with clothing—hence their nearly constant value as proportions of expenditure over the time series Halbwachs examined. One regrets that his idea about the social structuring of pressures to consume was not pursued with more energy, for it is still a necessary corrective for individualistic thinking in the theory of demand. Likewise, the sociological definition of class, based on shared values, is good; but reading *La Classe ouvrière* one is impressed with what it does not say. It is fair enough that in 1913 he should have found the individualist assumptions of utility theory inadequate. It is only a pity, given his mathematical training, that he did not recognize that utility theory is not really a philosophy to be disproved by philosophical arguments. It is the philosophical support of an operational device which works well enough not to be discarded until a correspondingly powerful mathematical apparatus can be offered to do the same analytic tasks equally well. Consequently, Halbwachs missed out on the real dialogue about tools of analysis which preoccupied the most brilliant thinkers in economics in his lifetime.

More worrying in this book is the shadow play with Marxist concepts. Josep Llobera has concluded, after much research, that the sociologists of *L'Année Sociologique*, like their British counterparts before and later, never took Marx's conceptual and theoretical contributions to their own subject seriously enough to warrant a sympathetic reading of his texts.[9] But this meticulous reinventing of alienation, false consciousness, and lumpen proletariat in Durkheimian terms suggests appropriation rather than ignorance. *Les Causes de suicide* is introduced by Mauss precisely as an updating of Durkheim's famous work of 1897. Halbwachs improves the statistical analyses, enlarges the data base, and generally confirms the value of the original insights. Like his other books, it is a disciple's tribute.

In 1930 Halbwachs visited the University of Chicago. *L'Évolution des besoins dans les classes ouvrières* came out in 1933 with analyses of a large number of budget surveys covering American as well as European households. A challenge to his earlier study, he found that among American workers the proportion of expenditure

---

[9] Josep R. Llobera, "Techno-Economic Determinism and the Work of Marx on Pre-Capitalist Societies," *Man*, June 1979, Vol. 14, No. 2, pp. 249–270.

on food had shown a marked downward trend. This should have led him to develop his earlier sociological theory of demand by calling for empirical data on possible changes in the social environment of American working-class families. Presumably, the changed pattern of expenditure should have lead him to seek signs of less isolation, less fragmentation, less frustration in the American workers' households. He could have developed his theory of thirty years earlier by connecting it to the relative absence of restrictive social effects in American life and class structure, which in Europe were causing the workers' search for esteem to stop at the immediate family and the street-life society. Instead, he weakly argued from his initial assumptions that the isolation, fragmentation, etc., of the American worker had kept him ignorant and consequently vulnerable to the wiles of advertisers in the new technology, so that he bought vacuum cleaners and improved his own house when his income rose. Likewise, in *Analyse des mobiles* (1938), and *La Morphologie sociale* (1938), Halbwachs remained uncritically faithful to an inflexible model of working-class collective representations. His comprehensive 1940 survey of international work on sociology, economics, and demography (for *Actualités Scientifiques et Industrielles*) is an extraordinary revelation of how isolated from other thinkers the *Année Sociologique* group had become in the interwar period. The review covers all that was important and contemporary in those growing fields. In economics Halbwachs concludes his competent summary of Keynesian theory with a competent account of Joan Robinson's criticism. He seems to be perfectly in touch with his colleagues abroad. Such reviews are intended to facilitate transmission of ideas across continents and seas. But when such an able scholar with a particular trained bias summarizes a foreign corpus of work, the effect is to break the circuit. No one reading that review in France would feel any need to take the Keynesian argument too seriously, for the reviewer ends by dismissing it on the authority of François Simiand's vague disparagements. In 1935 Halbwachs had become a member of the International Institute of Statistics. Clearly he was interested and capable in sociological analysis, but he never made his best contribution in this direction. His regular reviews of economics and demography for *L'Année Sociologique* were laconic and dull. The sharply critical, idealistic tone of his two early essays on Paris was so different that one presumes that his voice in this area was muffled by editorial policy.

To turn from this to his work on memory is refreshing. *Les Cadres sociaux de la mémoire* (1925) was the starting point. In the first part he distinguishes dreams from memory. Discussing Bergson and Freud, he defines dreams as individual fragments of experience. The defining character of memories, as distinct from dreams, is that memories are supported by those of others; they are public and shareable. He emphasizes the importance of spatial memory for locating memories of past experiences. The body of the book examines how different social segments, each with a different historical past, will have different memories attached to their respective landmarks. The book was attacked because he brushed aside individual psychology and insisted that even our most personal feelings and thoughts arise in social situations. His critics felt the threat of sociological determinism. He answered these criticisms much later in *The Collective Memory*. To his claim that there are no individual intuitions or memories, a challenger declared: Even if you claim that ninety-nine percent of memory is reconstructed and only one percent is real individual recall, this one percent gives enough basis for questioning the importance you assign to the social processes in remembering. But Halbwachs is steadfast, as his response shows. Even the child's world is never empty of human beings, benign or malevolent, still less the adult's world. Even a solitary perception of being alone is itself a recognition of the state of being in society. In reply to his critics he confirms one of their suspicions, as he comes out emphatically in favor of social determinism. Referring to Bergson's theory that we have an intuition of a unified consciousness, Halbwachs retorts: We think our consciousness is unified, this is an illusion; just as we think our actions are undetermined, they are not.

Les Cadres sociaux de la mémoire is programmatic, somewhat of a manifesto. One could call the two works that followed applied exercises demonstrating the value of the program. The first is a short essay on the collective memory of musicians (1939). The second is a book on the Christian memory of its holy places, *La Topographie légendaire des évangiles en terre sainte* (1941). The first considers remembering processes which essentially do not have spatial orientations; the second considers how the spatial framework of memory is continually deformed and remade according to the changing concerns of the living people who do the remembering.

Since the essay on musical memory is reprinted at the end of this volume, there would seem to be little need to say much about it here. But of all Halbwachs' works it is the most widely known today, as it was summarized by Alfred Schutz in his much reproduced essay "Making Music Together" (1951). Unfortunately for Halbwachs' modern reputation, Schutz's account is grossly inaccurate. A close reading of both essays reveals strong sympathy between them. Their only serious disagreement is on the question of innate ideas, brought into prominence by Schutz's loyalty to Bergson. Natural allies are often separated by sectarian disdain. In this case, Schutz's curt "So much for Halbwachs" is the harsher because in the forty years since "La Mémoire collective chez les musiciens" first appeared phenomonology and cognate disciplines for exploring consciousness followed the directions where Halbwachs led. Where else could they go by inspired combinations of observation and introspection?

Let me use David Sudnow's remarkable book on learning to play jazz as an illustration of the points that Halbwachs makes. *Ways of the Hand: The Organization of Improvised Conduct* (1978) is a study that fits just as well in the positivist tradition developed by Halbwachs as in the ethnomethodological tradition of Garfinkel, the acknowledged teacher, and of Harvey Sacks, to whom it is dedicated.

First, Halbwachs wants to convince the reader that remembering music is a difficult feat. He insists that the isolated individual could not do it, a claim that Schutz finds absurd. It is particularly difficult because musical notes are not connected with anything but each other. They do not signify solid objects or events, which can act as triggers to the memory. As Suzanne Langer said, Music has all the earmarks of a true symbolism except one: the existence of an assigned connotation.[10] Music unfolds in its own musical medium. The puzzle of remembering music is an acute form of Durkheim's problem about how religious cults persist in the minds of their worshippers without a physical, visible point of reference. Halbwachs remarks that all students of music make private schemata for remembering tunes, recognizing patterns in the timing, intervals, and rhythms. Without such schemata nothing would be recalled at all. This private symbolizing, the first effort to remember music, does not achieve very much. It becomes easier if the hearing can be accompanied by reproduction, singing, for example, so that movements in the brain are supplemented by movements in the larynx, which register further movements in the brain to carry the pattern in memory. Remembering becomes still easier if there are words and rhymes and associated ideas which support the faltering musical memory by nonmusical props. Best of all is the written score, which gives a spatialized summary of the music, a visible support. If music were not a social activity, it could not be remembered and so could not exist: the more the community is intensively specialized for music the stronger the attention and the richer the range of their remembering. Musicians, lay or professional, can only achieve their appropriate level of musical experience by making music together.

Schutz would disagree on the difficulty for an isolated individual of remembering music. But Sudnow says:

> I got a first taste for the magnitude of the problems I was in for when I tried to listen to a piece of jazz melody on a record and then go to the piano to play it. . . Even when taking a portion of a melody from a record where I thought I knew the improvised section well (and it is worth noting that the existence of the recording gives improvised melodies a status they would otherwise not have that they can be heard and learned as 'fixed melodies'), a symptomatic vagueness in my grasp of these familiar improvisations was discovered. I knew these melodies only in certain broad outlines. . . . I had been glossing the particularities of the notes in many of my hummings,

[10] Susanne Langer, *Philosophy in a New Key: A Study in the Symbolism of Reason, Rite and Art*, Harvard University Press, 1942.

grasping their essential shape perhaps, but not singing them with refined pitch sensitivity.[11]

When it comes to trying to remember a tune, Halbwachs says that we represent tunes in symbols "*a notre manière.*"[12] Sudnow draws elegant trajectories of his own to remind himself of different rhythmic styles. All through the apprenticeship he is describing, his teacher is in the background giving his weekly lessons, and Jimmy Rowles is in the foreground, the model jazz pianist, along with the other players, even when he was practicing alone:

> Every once in a while the time would get into the fingers as I sat and tried to move like Jimmy Rowles, setting a beat first by getting my shoulders going around a little, while I tapped my foot and snapped my fingers before play; counting off the time with a care I had never taken before, a care for the jazz to be played, a care for the others with whom I could have been coordinating my moves, for that bass player and drummer who were never around, that we might stride into the song together. . . .[13]

Like Halbwachs, Sudnow assumes that music is a language to be laboriously learned by social processes:

> I learned this language through five years of overhearing it spoken. I had come to learn, overhearing and overseeing this jazz as my instructable hands' ways—in a terrain nexus of hands and keyboard whose respective surfaces had become known as the respective surfaces of my tongue and teeth and palate are known to each other— that this jazz music *is* ways of moving from place to place as singing with my fingers. To define jazz (as to define any phenomenon of human action) is to *describe* the body's ways.[14]

Such lyricism is beyond Halbwachs' style, but the hard and lucid analysis conveys exactly his message about the physical, spatial, and social elements in learning.

Shortly after this, Halbwachs turned his attention to the spatial

[11] David Sudnow, *Ways of the Hand: The Organization of Improvised Conduct*, Harvard University Press, 1978.
[12] "La Mémoire collective chez les musiciens," p. 171.
[13] Sudnow, p. 141.
[14] Ibid., p. 179.

aspects of memory. The phenomenologist disagreeing with his declared determinism would have done well to challenge Halbwachs here, because his analysis never allows him to suggest that spatial orderings of memory fix it for good and all. Quite the contrary, they are elements used by human intentions one way in one decade and quite differently when social concerns have changed in another decade; the holy places revered by Christians in Palestine shift according to historically significant doctrinal and political changes. *La Topographie légendaire des évangiles en terre sainte* is a very careful empirical study, following in the steps of Renan, that strives to identify the original spots revered in Christian tradition, and finds some lost, some duplicated many times over, and some clearly wrong. Halbwachs adds his own surmises to make sense of the pattern on the ground as remembered, after the rebuilding of Jerusalem, after the discovery of the true cross by Constantine's mother, and other shifts of cultic enthusiasm.

These two studies represent a big effort toward empirical demonstration of this positivist sociologist's main work. What is amazing is that Halbwachs never thought of more exact methods of testing and never seems to have had any relation with his renowned contemporary, Frederick Bartlett, who spent his life contriving clever laboratory tests for memory. Halbwachs had far richer ideas than Bartlett, though the latter actually claimed to be looking for a sociological approach to memory.[15] It is not difficult to imagine experiments with musical memory and spatial memory that these pioneers could have worked out together. But in this case Halbwachs was not the circuit breaker. The author of a famous book on *Remembering* could hardly omit any reference to his contemporary colleague's work, but his account of the assumptions and conclusions of the *L'Année Sociologique* group is almost as disdainful and quite as misleading as that by Schutz.

In Bartlett's travestied account, Halbwachs is dismissed for accepting from Durkheim a unitary conception of society and for reifying collective memory into a quasi-mystic soul with its own ex-

---

[15] F.C. Bartlett, *Remembering: A Study in Experimental and Social Psychology*, Cambridge University Press, 1932.

istence. According to Bartlett, Durkheim "believes that the social group constitutes a genuine psychical unit, and is possessed of nearly all the characteristics of the human individual." He struggles to distinguish memory in the group, which he regards as a legitimate concept, from an illegitimate idea of the "memory of the group" which he wrongly foists upon Halbwachs.[16] This is particularly unfair, as readers of *The Collective Memory* will realize.

Halbwachs' gift to Durkheim was to unpack and separate clearly the elements of social life that contribute to the collective memory. His concept was of a flexible, articulated set of social segments consisting of live individuals who sustain their common interests by their own selective and highly partial view of history. This is not only in accord with modern analyses of ideological forgetting, structural amnesia, and theoretical blindspots in science, but it is an achievement which has been largely responsible for contemporary sophistication on the subject. To have worked this out within the strong constraints evidently imposed by Durkheim on his colleagues was a signal service to Durkheim himself and a contribution to Durkheim studies.

No wonder that Halbwachs wanted to write, in his late sixties, one more book on the collective memory—a synthesis and final justification. Friends close to him expected an important contribution and deplored his untimely end, as much for the interruption of this work as for the crime and sorrow of his deportation and death in Buchenwald. Indeed, it is an important synthesis and it shows extraordinary advances on his preceding work.

Much of the book contains criticisms of Bergsonism with support from Leibnitz. All the discussion of the private experience of pain; whether time can be conceived as passing more quickly for some people than for others; the concept of a universal, empty time frame encompassing all existences, solipsist problems arising from a concept of subjective inner time experience—these are all aimed against Bergson's subjectivist theory of knowledge. They are good arguments; phenomenologists have the opportunity here of deciding

[16] Ibid., Ch. 18, paragraph 2.

whether they need to carry that particular philosophical burden of innate ideas in order to follow the important new programs of research which propose themselves as soon as human intentions are taken as the initial point of departure.

When it comes to the concept of time as used by mathematicians, Halbwachs used Bergson's own account with approval. Mathematical time is an attempt to enlarge and universalize time; it is a uniform perception like the geometrization of space. Historians' use of time is again very different from the ordinary experience of individuals. Historians create historical time periods which have meaning for their professional concern with tracing synchronies and sequences, but have no correspondence with any historical experience anyone ever lived through, no anchorage in any collective memory. No one arrives at the dawn of a great historical period exclaiming, Today we begin the Hundred Years War! The argument expresses a deep debt to Bergson; it is not always critical. The most significant Bergsonian idea is the conflation of the future and the past in the present. Interspersed with the dialogue with Bergson are the rich insights into the social reconstruction of history, the elliptical collapse of long periods of time when nothing significant is observed to happen, the social structuring of time, and other important insights. The memory of a society, he said, goes back only as far as it can; that is, it goes back as far as the memory of its constituent groups. Vast quantities of information are forgotten, not from spite or intention, but merely because the groups which used to remember them have disappeared. The divisions of time in the collective memory correspond to the divisions of society. Whereas this message has been received and accepted by sociologists and historians, the use made of it has been partial and ad hoc. It has fallen to anthropologists to develop the simultaneous analysis of the structures of a society and the structure of its experience of time and to consider their respective time frameworks as bases for comparing historical societies.[17]

---

[17] For an exemplary case study, see E. E. Evans-Pritchard, *Nuer*, Oxford University Press, 1940. And for a summary of references to subsequent work, *Evans-Pritchard* by Mary Douglas, Modern Masters Series, Fontana Viking, 1980.

Jean Duvignaud, in his preface to the first edition, wrote that time recollected was a specially important cultural theme in the first quarter of this century. He cited Proust, Joyce, and Henry James as novelists experimenting with new uses of memory's perspectives; he also cited Freud in psychology and Einstein in physics. He introduced Halbwachs as one having taken up that contemporary theme and having so well adapted sociological thinking in this respect to an Einsteinian relativism that nothing can be said on the subject of memory now that does not owe him a debt. Let this be my conclusion too and let the book speak for itself.

MAURICE HALBWACHS' PRINCIPAL PUBLICATIONS

1907   *Leibniz*, Les Philosophes.

1908   "La Politique foncière des municipalités," *Les Cahiers Socialiste*, No. 3, pp. 3-32.

1909   "Les Expropriations et le prix des terrains à Paris, 1860-1900." Revised version published 1928 as "La Population et les tracés des voies à Paris depuis cent ans."

1913   *La Classe ouvrière et les niveaux de vie: recherches sur la hierarchie des besoins dans les sociétés industrielles contemporaines.* (Primary doctoral dissertation.)

1913   *La Théorie de l'homme moyen: essai sur Quetelet et la statistique morale.* (Secondary doctoral dissertation.)

1924   *Le Calcul des probabilités à la portée de tous.* Co-author with M. Frechet.

1924   *Les Origines du sentiment religieux d'après Durkheim.* Paris: F. Alcan. English translation published 1962 as *Sources of Religious Sentiment.* The Free Press.

1925   *Les Cadres sociaux de la mémoire*, Les Travaux de L'Année Sociologique. Paris: F. Alcan. Republished 1952 by Presses Universitaires de France.

1928   "La Population et les tracés de voies à Paris depuis cents ans." (Revised version of 1909 article.)

1930   *Les Causes de suicide*, Les Travaux de L'Année Sociologique. Foreword by Marcel Mauss. Paris: F. Alcan. English translation published 1978 as *The Causes of Suicide.* The Free Press.

1933   *L'Evolution des besoins dans les classes ouvrières.* Paris: F. Alcan.

1938   *Analyse des mobiles qui orientent l'activité des individus dans la vie sociale.* Republished 1952 as *Esquisse d'une psychologie des classes sociales.* Introduction by George Friedmann. Presses Universitaires de France. English translation published 1958 as *Psychology of Social Classes.* The Free Press.

1938   *La Morphologie sociale.* Presses Universitaires de France. English translation published as *Population and Society: Introduction to Social Morphology.* The Free Press.

1939   "La Mémoire collective chez les musiciens," *Revue philosophique*, pp. 136-165.

1940   "Sociologie économique et demographie," Philosophie: 9, *Actualités Scientifiques et Industrielles.*

1941   *La Topographie légendaire des évangiles en terre sainte: étude de mémoire collective.* Presses Universitaires de France.

1950   *La Mémoire collective.* Preface by Jean Duvignaud. Introduction by Michel Alexandre. Presses Universitaires de France. English translation published 1980 as *The Collective Memory.* Introduction by Mary Douglas. Harper & Row.

1. Individual Memory and Collective Memory

Comparing Testimony

We appeal to witnesses to corroborate or invalidate.as well as supplement what we somehow know already about an event that in many other details remains obscure. One witness we can always call on is ourself. When a person says, I don't believe my own eyes, he feels himself two beings. A sensory being comes to testify like a witness to what it has seen before a self which has not presently seen what is in question, but which may have seen it in the past or formed an opinion from the testimony of others. When we return to a city previously visited, what we perceive helps us to restore a picture, certain portions of which had been forgotten. If what we currently see fits into the framework of our old memories, the converse is also true, for these memories adapt to the mass of present perceptions. It is as if we were comparing the testimony of several witnesses. In spite of discrepancies, they agree on the essentials that permit us to reconstruct a body of remembrances that we recognize.

Our confidence in the accuracy of our impression increases, of course, if it can be supported by others' remembrances also. It is as if the very same experience were relived by several persons instead of only one. When we meet a friend after a long separation, we at first have difficulty re-establishing contact with him. However, as we recall together various circumstances related to the same events, recollections that may not agree, haven't we managed to think and remember in common and don't past events stand out more sharply? Don't we believe that we relive the past more fully because we no longer represent it alone, because we see it now as we saw it then, but through the eyes of another as well?

Our memories remain collective, however, and are recalled to us through others even though only we were participants in the events or saw the things concerned. In reality, we are never alone. Other men need not be physically present, since we always carry with us and in us a number of distinct persons. I arrive for the first time in London and take walks with different companions. An architect directs my attention to the character and arrangement of city buildings. A historian tells me why a certain street, house, or other spot is historically noteworthy. A painter alerts me to the colors in the parks, the lines of the palaces and churches, and the play of light and shadow on the walls and façades of Westminster and on the Thames. A businessman takes me into the public thoroughfares, to the shops, bookstores, and department stores. Even if I were unaccompanied, I need only have read their varying descriptions of the city, been given advice on what aspects to see, or merely studied a map. Now suppose I went walking alone. Could it be said that I preserve of that tour only individual remembrances, belonging solely to me? Only in appearance did I take a walk alone. Passing before Westminster, I thought about my historian friend's comments (or, what amounts to the same thing, what I have read in history books). Crossing a bridge, I noticed the effects of perspective that were pointed out by my painter friend (or struck me in a picture or engraving). Or I conducted my tour with the aid of a map. Many impressions during my first visit to London—St. Paul's, Mansion House, the Strand, or the Inns of Court—reminded me of Dickens' novels read in childhood, so I took my walk with Dickens. In each of these moments I cannot say that I was alone, that I reflected alone, because I had put myself in thought into this or that group, composed of myself and the architect (or, beyond him, the group for which he was merely the interpreter), the painter (or his group), the land surveyor who had designed the layout of the city, or the novelist. Other men have had these remembrances in common with me. Moreover, they help me to recall them. I turn to these people, I momentarily adopt their viewpoint, and I re-enter their group in order to better remember. I can still feel the group's influence and recognize in myself many ideas and ways of thinking that could not have originated with me and that keep me in contact with it.

Forgetting Due to Separation from a Group

Witnesses in the ordinary sense of the word—individuals physically present to the senses—are therefore not necessary to confirm or recall a remembrance. Moreover, they would never be sufficient. By putting together remembrances, several people (or even one) may be able to describe very accurately facts or things that we ourselves viewed also, even to reconstitute the entire sequence of our actions and words in definite circumstances, while we are unable to recall anything of all this. That is, the facts may be indisputable. We are shown beyond any doubt that a certain event occurred, that we were present and actively participated in it. Nevertheless this episode remains foreign to us, just as though someone else played our role.

Let us revert to an example that has been raised in opposition to my views. There have been in our life a certain number of events that had to happen. It is certain that there was a first day that I attended *lycée*, a first day I entered the third or fourth grade. Although this fact can be located in time and space, and even though my parents or friends provide me an accurate account of it, I am in the presence of an abstract datum to which I cannot make any living remembrance correspond—I recall nothing about it. Or I no longer recognize some place that I have assuredly passed by several times or some person whom I certainly met. Nevertheless, the witnesses are present. Therefore, is their role wholly incidental and complementary, doubtlessly useful to me in specifying and supplementing my remembrances, but only if these have already reappeared and therefore been preserved in my mind? But there is nothing in this that should surprise anyone. The fact that I have witnessed or participated in an episode at which others were spectators or participants is never sufficient reason that later on, when they evoke that event for me and reconstitute its image bit by bit, this artificial construction suddenly takes life and becomes transformed into a remembrance. Very often, it is true, such images imposed on us by our milieu change the impression that we have kept of some distant fact, or of some person known long ago. It might be that such images reproduce the past inaccurately, while that element or fragment of remembrance already in our mind is a more accurate expression: in this case a solid fund of fictitious remembrances is added to real remembrances. Conversely, it is possible that only the testimony of others is accurate and that they rectify and re-establish our remembrances in the process of being incorporated into it. In both cases these images blend into our remembrances and seemingly lend them their own substance because our memory is not a blank tablet and we feel able to perceive in them, as in a distorted mirror, features and contours (illusory perhaps) providing us an image of the past. Just as we must introduce a small particle into a saturated medium to get crystallization, so must we introduce a "seed" of memory into that body of testimony external to us in order for it to turn into a solid mass of remembrances. If, on the contrary, this episode has apparently left, as is said, "no trace in our memory"—that is, if we feel entirely incapable of reconstructing any portion of it in the absence of this external evidence—then those who describe it to us may paint a living picture that nonetheless will never become a remembrance.

Moreover, when I state that testimony will recall nothing if no trace of the past event in question remains in our mind, I do not mean that the remembrance or some part of it has to continue to exist as such in us. I only mean that, from the moment when we and these other witnesses belong to the same group and think in common about these matters, we maintain contact with this group and remain capable of identifying ourselves with it and merging our past with its. Putting it another way, we must from this moment on never have lost the habit and capacity to think and remember as a member of the group to which we all belonged, to place ourself in its viewpoint and employ the conceptions shared by its members.

Consider a professor who has taught for fifteen years at a *lycée*. He encounters one of his former pupils and hardly recognizes him. The student speaks of his old classmates, recalling where each had to sit in class. He evokes many incidents that took place in his class during that year, including the achievements of certain students, the peculiarities or inadequacies of others, portions of certain courses, and certain explanations that particularly interested or caught the fancy of the students. Even though the pupil's recollections are accurate, it is quite likely that the professor has kept no remembrance of any of this. Moreover, during that school year, the professor was unquestionably very aware of the character of this class. He could recognize each student and knew about all the events and incidents that altered, accelerated, disturbed, or slowed the rhythm of life of this class, ensuring it a history of its own. How could he have forgotten all that? And how does it happen that, with the exception of a few vague reminiscences, the words of his former pupil raise no echoes of that time in his memory? The group constituting a class is essentially ephemeral, at least if it is considered to include teacher as well as students. It is no longer the same class when the pupils, perhaps the same individuals, pass from one class to another and sit in different seats. At year's end the students scatter, and this distinct and particular class will never come together again. Nevertheless, an important distinction must be made. For the pupils, the class lives on for some time. At least they will have many occasions to think about and remember it. Being nearly the same age, they may belong to the same social circles and will not forget being together under the same teacher. The concepts that he has taught them bear his imprint. Thinking again about this or that concept, they often perceive the teacher who first presented it to them, as well as their classmates who shared its reception. For the teacher, the situation is quite different. In class he carried out his function. The technical aspect of his activity is the same for all such classes. In effect, the teacher repeats the same course, and each year of teaching is not so clearly contrasted to any other as each year is for the students. His instruction—from his exhortations, reprimands, and expressions of sympathy for each student to his gestures, accent, and even his jokes—is new to his students, but may be for him only a series of habitual actions deriving from his occupation. None of this can be the basis of a body of remembrances relevant to any specific class. There exists no durable group to which the professor continues to belong, about which he might have occasion to think, and within whose viewpoint he could resituate himself to remember with it the past.

But this is the case whenever others reconstruct for us events that we have lived through with them, but about which we can recreate no feeling of *déjà vu*. There is a discontinuity between these events, the others engaged in them, and ourself. It arises not solely from the fact that the group in whose midst we perceived the events no longer physically exists, but also because we no longer think about them or have the means to reconstruct an image of them. In our eyes, each member of that group was defined by his place amid the others and not by his relationships (of which we were ignorant) to other social circles. All the remembrances that might originate within the professor's class had to be supported by one another and not on external remembrances. The duration of such a memory was thus limited by the force of things to the duration of the group. If witnesses nevertheless remain—if, for example, former pupils recall and try to recall to their professor what he does not remember—it is because they formed in class with fellow students or outside class with their relatives various little communities, more intimate and certainly more durable than the class itself. Classroom events interested all these smaller groups, affected them, and left their mark upon them. But the professor was excluded from these groups—or, at least, if the members of these groups included him, he was not aware of it.

It often happens that one member of a group misjudges what the other members think of him. Such variations in viewpoint are the source of many misunderstandings and disappointments. Examples may be found in all types of groups. Let us consider emotional relationships, in which imagination plays a prominent role. A person who is deeply loved but does not reciprocate in kind often becomes aware too late, if at all, of the importance attached to his smallest acts and his most insignificant words. He who has the greater love will remind the beloved of declarations and promises that the latter made but no longer remembers. Usually the beloved in such cases has not been deceitful, inconsiderate, or capricious but has merely been less caught up than the other in this relationship, which rested on an uneven distribution of sentiments. Thus a very religious man, whose life was so exemplary that he was beatified after his death, might well be astonished were he to return to life and read the legends about himself. Nonetheless, those legends were composed with the help of remembrances preciously preserved and faithfully written down by those among whom he lived that portion of his life recounted in them. Many of these recorded events would not be recognized by the saint himself because they never happened to begin with. But others might always have escaped his notice because he was then absorbed in his inner image of God, and only those about him focused their attention upon him.

A person might be as interested as others (maybe more so) in an event, however, and still preserve no remembrance of it. He fails to recognize that event even after it has been described to him because, soon after its occurrence, he left and never returned to the group in which the event had attracted his notice. It is said of certain persons that they live solely in the present. That is, they are concerned only with those persons and things related to their current activities, interests, or occupation. They forget about associates once a business deal has been closed, or about traveling companions once the trip is over. They are immediately absorbed by other interests and into other groups. A sort of vital impulse drives their thoughts from whatever might interfere with present concerns. By force of circumstances, such persons may go full circle, passing back and forth through the same groups much as in old dances, in which one constantly changes partners only to periodically regain a former partner. Similarly, these people leave a group only to re-enter it later on. In the process they might be said to recover their remembrances of all these groups because their capacity to forget works alternately to the advantage and then to the detriment of each. But eventually these people who live in the present may follow a path that does not cut across paths traveled earlier but, instead, gradually takes them further away. If, later on, they should encounter members of these now unfamiliar groups, they try in vain to find their way back to and reconstitute the old group. It is much like following a previously traveled route, but doing it in a roundabout way so that the route is now viewed from places from which it had never been seen before. The various details are resituated in a different whole, constituted by our momentary representations. It seems as if a new route has been taken. Indeed details could acquire their old meaning only in relation to a totally different whole that our thought no longer embraces. We could recall all these details in their appropriate order, but we must have this whole as the point of departure. This is no longer possible, however, because we have long been remote from it and would have to backtrack too far.

Such loss of memory resembles that type of amnesia in which a clearly defined and limited body of remembrances is forgotten. It has been confirmed that a person who has received a severe blow to the brain may forget a whole period of his past, usually from just before the blow back to some date beyond which he has normal recall. Alternatively, all the remembrances belonging to a certain category are forgotten, regardless of when they were acquired. Loss of a specific foreign language would be an example of this. These cases seem to be adequately explained from a physiological viewpoint, not as a consequence of remembrances of a given period or category being localized in that part of the brain injured but as a result of damage to the cerebral function of remembering as a whole. The brain ceases to perform only certain operations, just as an organism might be temporarily unable to walk, speak, or digest food without any other function being impaired. But it could equally well be said that what is damaged is the general capacity to enter into relationship with the groups making up society. The individual becomes separated from one or more groups and only from these.

The whole body of remembrances that we share in common with them suddenly disappears. To forget a period of one's life is to lose contact with those who then surrounded us. To forget a foreign language is to no longer have the power to comprehend those who speak to us in that language, living persons or authors whose works we read. When we turned toward them, we adopted a definite attitude, just as we do in the presence of any human grouping. It is no longer within our control to adopt this attitude and to turn toward that group. Suppose we now encounter someone who certifies that we have learned a certain language. Reading our books and notes, he finds evidence on each page that we translated text and that we knew how to apply the proper rules. None of this suffices to re-establish the interrupted contact between ourself and all those who speak or write that language. We no longer possess enough attentive force to sustain contact with both this group and others with which we have more recently and intimately been concerned. Moreover, there is no reason to be surprised that only certain remembrances are suddenly abolished. They form an independent system because they are remembrances of the same group, interconnected and somehow mutually supporting. Since this group is clearly distinct from every other, we can simultaneously be in the others and outside this one. In a less abrupt and brutal fashion perhaps, and in the absence of any pathological disturbances, we gradually grow more remote and isolated from certain milieus not quite forgotten but only very vaguely remembered. We can still define in general terms groups with which we have been connected. But they no longer interest us because the whole character of our present life places them at a distance.

The Necessity of an Affective Community

Now suppose we took a trip with a group of companions whom we have not seen since. Our thoughts at the time were both very close and very far from them. We conversed with them and shared interest in the details of our route and various incidents during the trip. But, simultaneously, our reflections followed other paths unknown to them. We carried with us, in effect, feelings and ideas originating in other real or imaginary groups; we conversed inwardly with other persons. We peopled the passing landscape with other human beings, and a certain place or circumstance gained a value not present for our companions. Later on, we might encounter one of our traveling companions. He refers to certain particulars of the voyage that he remembers. We too would remember these details had we remained in contact with our companions and shared their subsequent conversations. But we have forgotten everything that he evokes and endeavors in vain to make us remember. By contrast, we recall what we then experienced unknown to the others, as if this type of remembrance had left a much deeper imprint in our memory because it concerned only ourself. Thus, in this example, the testimony of others is powerless to reconstitute a forgotten remembrance and, on the other hand, we remember, apparently without the support of others, impressions that we have communicated to no one.

Does this analysis lead to the conclusion that individual memory, to the extent that it is contrasted to collective memory, is a necessary and sufficient condition for the recall and recognition of remembrances? Not at all. That first remembrance is obliterated and can no longer be retrieved because we have not belonged for some time to the group in whose memory it is conserved. To be aided by others' memory, ours must not merely be provided testimony and evidence but must also remain in harmony with theirs. There must be enough points of contact so that any remembrance they recall to us can be reconstructed on a common foundation. A remembrance is gained not merely by reconstituting the image of a past event a piece at a time. That reconstruction must start from shared data or conceptions. These are present in our mind as well as theirs, because they are continually being passed back and forth. This process occurs only because all have been and still are members of the same group. This is the only way to understand how a remembrance is at once recognized and reconstructed. What does it matter that our companions are still influenced by a feeling that we once experienced with them but do no longer? We can't evoke it because we have shared nothing with our former companions for so long. There is nothing to fault in our memory or theirs. But a larger collective memory, encompassing both ours and theirs, has disappeared.

Similarly, men who have been brought close together—for example, by a shared task, mutual devotion, common ancestry, or artistic endeavor—may disperse afterwards into various groups. Each new group is too restricted to retain everything that concerned the thoughts of the original party, literary coterie, or religious congregation. So each fastens onto one facet of its thought and remembers only part of its activities. Several pictures of that common past are thus generated, none being really accurate or coinciding with any other. Once they are separated, not one of them can reproduce the total content of the original thought. If two such groups come back into contact, what they lack in order to mutually encompass, understand, and confirm remembrances of that past common life is precisely the capacity to forget the barriers dividing them. A misunderstanding weighs upon them, much as upon two men who meet once again only to find, as is said, that they no longer "speak the same language."

What about the fact that we remember impressions that none of our companions could have known about at the time? This in itself is no more a proof of our memory being self-sufficient and without need of the support of others' memories. Suppose that at the time we begin a trip with a group of friends, we are vitally concerned with some matter they know nothing about. Since we are absorbed in our ideas and feelings, everything seen or heard is related to it. We nourish our secret thought from everything in the field of perception that can be connected with it. It is as if we had never left that distant group of human beings who are the basis for our concern. We incorporate into that group every element assimilable from our new milieu. By contrast, we hold to the new milieu, considered in itself and from the viewpoint of our companions, with the least significant part of ourself. If we think about that trip later on, we cannot say that we placed ourself within the viewpoint of those who made the trip with us. We recall them only as their persons were included in the framework of our concerns. Similarly, when at dusk we entered a room for the first time, we saw the walls, furniture, and furnishings through a shadow of darkness. These fantastic and mysterious shapes are retained in our memory as a barely real framework for those feelings of uneasiness, surprise, or sadness we experienced at that first view of the room. Seeing the room in daylight is not enough to recall them to us. We must also think about those feelings we then experienced. Was it, therefore, our personal response that so transfigured these objects for us? Yes, if you prefer—but only on condition that we do not forget that our most personal feelings and thoughts originate in definite social milieus and circumstances. The effect of that contrast resulted primarily from the fact that we sought, in these objects, not what was seen by those familiar with them, but what was related to the concerns of those persons through whose thoughts we saw that room the first time.

On the Possibility of a Strictly Individual Memory

If this analysis is correct, its conclusions may permit a reply to the most serious and, moreover, most natural objection to the theory that a person remembers only by situating himself within the viewpoint of one or several groups and one or several currents of collective thought.

It may be conceded that a great many of our remembrances reappear because other persons recall them to us. Even in those instances when others are not physically present and we evoke an event that had a place in the life of our group, it might be granted that we can speak of collective memory because we once envisaged that event, as we still do now in the moment we recall it, from the viewpoint of this group. We are certainly justified in requesting agreement with this second point, because such a mental attitude is possible only for a person who belongs (or has belonged) to a group and thus still feels, even at a distance, its influence. The fact that we could think about a certain object only because we act as a member of a group is sufficient reason to state that an obvious condition of that thought is the existence of the group. Hence, a person returning home by himself has undoubtedly spent some time "all alone," as the saying goes. But he has been alone in appearance only, because his thoughts and actions during even this period are explained by his nature as a social being and his not having ceased for one instant to be enclosed within some group. The difficulty does not rest here.

But don't some remembrances reappear that can in no way be connected with a group? The events they reproduce would be perceived by ourself when we were really and not only apparently alone. Such remembrances would not be resituated within the thought of any body of individuals, and we would recall them by placing ourself within a viewpoint that could only be our own. Even were instances of this type very rare or even exceptional, the verification of just a few would establish that the collective memory does not account for all our remembrances and, perhaps, cannot alone explain the evocation of any remembrance. After all, given our analysis, it could be that all these conceptions and images that derive from our social groups and operate in the memory lie like a screen over the individual remembrance, even in those cases when we never become aware of that remembrance. The whole point is to know if such a remembrance could exist, if it is conceivable. The fact that it occurs, even if only once, suffices to prove that nothing opposes its operation in every case. There would then be, at the basis of every remembrance, the recollection of a purely individual conscious state that, in order to distinguish it from perceptions permeated by elements of social thought, could be called a "sensory intuition."

As Charles Blondel has written:

We experience some uneasiness to see totally (or almost totally) eliminated from remembering any glimmer of that *sensory intuition* which, while not the sum total, is very evidently the essential prelude and condition sine qua non of perception. . . . For us to avoid confusing the reconstitution of our own proper past with that which we can fabricate from the past of our fellow men, in order for this empirically, logically, and socially possible past to become indentified with our real past, certain parts must be something more than a mere reconstitution of borrowed materials.[1]

Désiré Roustan has written to me:

If you content yourself to say that, when an individual thinks that he evokes the past, it is really ninety-nine percent reconstruction and one percent true evocation, that residue of one percent, which resists your explanation, suffices as a basis for the whole problem of the conservation of remembrances. Now, can you avoid that residual element?

Childhood Remembrances

Remembrances that take us back to a time when our sensations reflected only external objects, when we hadn't introduced images or thoughts connected with men and groups around us, are difficult to find. Indeed, we recall nothing of early childhood because our impressions could not fasten onto any support so long as we were not yet a social being. According to Stendhal:

The earliest remembrance that I have is biting the cheek or forehead of my cousin Madame Pison du Galland. . . a plump woman of twenty-five, who wore a great deal of rouge. . . . I can still see the whole scene, but that's probably because I was roundly chastised on the spot and never heard the end of it.[2]

Similarly, he recalls the day that he teased a mule, which then kicked him.

"A little more would have killed him," my grandfather used to say. I can picture the incident, but it is probably not a direct remembrance,

[1] Charles Blondel, "Critical Review" (of Maurice Halbwachs' *Les cadres sociaux de la mémoire*), *Revue philosophique 101* (1926), p. 296.

[2] Stendhal, *Vie d'Henri Brulard*, ed. Henri Martineau (Paris: Le Divan I, 1949), p. 36.

only a remembrance of the picture I formed of the matter a very long time ago, when I was first told about it.[3]

The same is true of most so-called childhood remembrances. The earliest that I have long considered myself able to retrieve is our arrival in Paris. I was ten and a half. We climbed the stairs to our fourth-floor apartment in the evening, and we children commented out loud that Paris meant living in a silo. Now perhaps one of us did make that remark. But our parents, who were amused, remembered the incident and recounted it to us later on. I can still picture our lighted staircase, but then I saw it many times after that first time.

Here is an event from the childhood of Benevenuto Cellini related at the beginning of his *Autobiography*. He is not certain that it is a remembrance. Nonetheless, we offer it as an aid to better understanding the example that follows, which we will thoroughly analyze.

> I was about three years old. My grandfather, Andréa Cellini, was still living and more than a hundred years old. One day while the pipe for the sink was being changed, a giant scorpion crept out of it. Unseen by the others, he got to the ground and hid under a bench. I saw it, ran to it, and picked it up. It was so big that its tail stuck out from one side of my hand while its claws stuck out at the other. I ran joyfully, so I am told, to my grandfather saying "Look, grandfather, at my beautiful little crayfish." He immediately recognized it as a scorpion and in his love for me, he almost died from fright. He begged me for it, with many caresses, but I held onto it all the more tightly, crying that I would not give it up to anyone. My father, who was in the house, came running at the outcry. Thunderstruck, he did not know how to take that venemous animal from me without its first killing me, when suddenly his eyes fell on a pair of scissors. Armed with them and coaxing me at the same time, he cut off the tail and the claws of the scorpion. Once the danger was over, he considered the episode a good omen.

This exciting and dramatic episode unfolded completely within the family. In picking up the scorpion, the child did not realize that

[3] Ibid., p. 62.

it was a dangerous animal. It was for him a small crayfish, like those his parents had shown him and let him touch, a kind of toy. In reality, a foreign element had penetrated into the home, and both grandfather and father reacted characteristically. The child's crying and the parents' comforting, caressing, anxiety, terror, and subsequent burst of joy constitute so many familial responses defining the meaning of the event. Even if we grant that the child recalls this episode, the image is still situated within the framework of the family, because it was initially enacted there and has never left it.

Let us now listen to Charles Blondel.

> I remember once, as a child, exploring an abandoned house and, in the middle of a dark room, suddenly falling up to my waist into a hole which had water at the bottom. I quite easily recognize when and where the thing occurred, but my knowing is totally subordinated in this case to my remembering.[4]

We are to understand that the remembrance occurs as an unlocalized image. He doesn't recall it, therefore, by thinking first about the house—that is, by placing himself in the viewpoint of the family living there. This is all the more true because, as Blondel says, he never told his parents about the incident nor has he thought about it since then. And he adds:

> In this instance, while I needed to reconstitute the environment of my remembrance, I by no means needed to reconstitute the remembrance itself. In memories of this kind, it seems correct to say that we have a direct contact with the past which precedes and conditions the historical reconstruction.[5]

This narrative is clearly different from the preceding. First of all, Cellini indicates the time and place of the episode he recalls, something Blondel is completely unaware of when he evokes his fall into a hole half full of water. Indeed Blondel stresses this very omission. Nonetheless, this may not be the essential difference between the two cases. The group to which the child at this age most intimately belongs, which constantly surrounds him, is the family. Now, in

[4] "Critical Review," p. 296.
[5] Ibid., pp. 296–297.

this instance, the child has left the family. Not only does he no longer see his parents, but he may not even have them in mind. At any rate, they do not intervene in this bit of history, either because they were not even informed about it or because they did not consider it important enough to retain and relate later on to him who had been its hero. But are these facts sufficient to state that he was truly alone? Is it true that the novelty and intensity of this impression— the distress of being abandoned and the strangeness and surprise in the face of the unexpected, of the unseen and unexperienced—explain his thought being diverted from his parents? On the contrary, did he not suddenly find himself in danger just because he was a child and so very dependent on adults in a network of domestic feelings and thoughts? But then he did think about his family and was alone in appearance only. It matters little that he doesn't recall the specific time and place of the incident and that it is not supported by a spatial and temporal framework. The thought of the absent family provides a framework, and the child need not, as Blondel says, "reconstitute the environment of my remembrance" because the remembrance arises within that environment. We should not be surprised that the child is unaware of it, that his attention did not focus at that moment on this aspect of his thought, or that he no longer notices it when he recalls as an adult that childhood remembrance. A "current of social thought" is ordinarily as invisible as the atmosphere we breathe. In normal life its existence is recognized only when it is resisted, but a child calling for and needing the help of his family is not resisting it.

Blondel might rightly object that the event he recalls is a set of particulars without any relationship to any aspect of his family. Exploring a dark room, he falls into a hole half full of water. Let us grant that he was frightened by being so far from his family. The essence of the fact, in comparison with which everything else seemingly fades to nothing, is this image that in itself occurs as totally detached from the domestic milieu. Now it is this image, and the perservation of this image, that must be explained. As such, this image is indeed distinguished from every other circumstance of my situation, either when I realized that I was far away from my family or when I turned to that group for help and toward that very "environment." In other words, it is not clear how a framework as general as the family could reproduce so particular a fact. As Blondel says, "There has to be a matter for these forms which are the collective frameworks imposed by society."[6]

Why not simply grant that this matter indeed exists and is nothing more than precisely what in the remembrances is without relation to the framework—that is, the sensations and sensory intuitions that are relived in that episode? When little Poucet was abandoned in the forest by his parents, he certainly thought about them; but he was also aware of many other things. He followed several paths, climbed a tree, saw a light, approached an isolated house, and so forth. How can all this be summarized in the simple comment that he was lost and couldn't find his parents? Had he taken other paths or had other encounters, his feeling of abandonment might have been the same, yet he would have kept totally different remembrances.

This is my answer. At the time a child becomes lost in a forest or a house, he is immersed only in the current of thoughts and feelings attaching him to family. As events proceed, it is as if he gets caught up in another current that removes him from it. Poucet could be said to remain within the family because he is in the company of his brothers. But he appoints himself leader, takes charge of them, and directs their activities. That is, he passes from the position of child to that of father, and he enters the group of adults while still a child. But something similar also applies to Blondel's remembrance. That memory belongs to both child and adult because the child was for the first time in an adult situation. When he was a child, all his thoughts were at a child's level. He was used to judging events by the standards his parents had taught him, and his surprise and fear were caused by his inability to relocate these new experiences in his little world. His own family no longer within reach, he became an adult in the sense that he found himself in the presence of novel and disturbing things (things that would certainly not have been so to the same extent for an adult). He may have stayed only moments in

[6] Ibid., p. 298.

that dark hole. But he made contact with a world that he would re-discover later, as he was allowed more freedom. Moreover, there are many instances throughout childhood when a child must con-front what is nonfamilial. For example, he may collide with or be injured by certain objects and thus learn to adjust to the various properties of things. He inevitably experiences a whole series of small tests, which are so many preparations for adulthood. This is the shadow that adult society projects over childhood. Sometimes it becomes far more than a shadow, as the child is called on to share the concerns and responsibilities that ordinarily fall on shoulders stronger than his own. Then he is temporarily and partially includ-ed in the group of adults. Hence it is said of certain people that they never had a childhood. Since they had to earn their livelihood too early in life, they entered the social struggle for existence at an age when most children are unaware that such places exist. Or they have known that type of suffering reserved for adults and have had to confront it on the same level as adults—e.g., after the death and burial of someone close.

The original content of such remembrances, which separates them from all others, is thus explained by the fact that they are found at the intersection of two or more series of thoughts, connect-ing them in turn to as many different groups. It is simply insuffi-cient to assert that what intersects with these series of thoughts link-ing us to a group (the family, in this case) is a series of sensations deriving from things. Everything would then become problematic once again, since this image of things would exist only for us and thus a portion of our remembrances would rest on no collective memory. But a child is afraid in the dark or when lost in a deserted place because he peoples that place with imaginary enemies, be-cause at night he fears bumping into all sorts of dangerous crea-tures. Rousseau tells how M. Lambercier gave him the key to the church one very dark autumn evening so that he could go look in the pulpit for a Bible that had been left there.

> On opening the door, I heard the echoings of what I thought were voices in the dome. My Roman resoluteness began to crumble. The door opened, I wanted to enter, but I had barely stepped in when I

stopped. Seeing the heavy darkness which pervaded that vast place, I was so terrified that my hair stood on end. I sat down confused on a bench. I no longer knew where I was. Unable to locate either the pulpit or the door, I was inexpressibly upset.

Had the church been lighted, he would have seen that no one was there and would not have been afraid. For the child the world is never empty of human beings, of good and evil influences. Perhaps more distinct images in our picture of the past correspond to these points where influences intersect because something we illuminate from two directions reveals more details and draws more of our attention.

Adult Remembrances

We have said enough about childhood remembrances. Adults can just as easily evoke many remembrances so original and so unified as to seemingly resist analysis. But we can always expose the same delusion in such examples. A given member of a group happens to also belong to another group. The thoughts from each suddenly come together in his mind. Presumably he alone perceives this contrast between them. Is it not obvious, therefore, that he has an impression unlike anything experienced by other members of these groups, whose only point of contact with each other is this individual? This remembrance is included at once in two frameworks. But each framework precludes the other's being seen. Concentrating his attention on their point of intersection, he is too preoccupied to perceive either of them distinctly. When we look in the sky for two stars belonging to different constellations, we readily imagine that by merely tracing an imaginary line between them we confer on them some sort of unity. Nevertheless, each is only an element in a group and we were able to recognize them because neither constellation was then hidden behind a cloud. Similarly, since two thoughts contrast and apparently reinforce one another when brought together, we think they form a self-existing whole, independent of their parent wholes. We fail to perceive that in reality we are considering the two groups simultaneously, but each from the viewpoint of the other.

Let us now revert to the hypothetical example examined previously. I made a trip with some people I had just met and whom I was not destined to see again for some time. It was a pleasure trip. I neither spoke nor listened very much. My mind was full of thoughts and images my companions were neither aware of nor interested in. People whom I loved and who shared my concerns were introduced unawares into this milieu. A whole community with which I was intimately linked was mingled with incidents and landscapes totally foreign or irrelevant to it. Let us consider my impression. It is undoubtedly explained by what dominated my intellectual and emotional life. But it still unfolded within a temporal and spatial framework. And it unfolded amid circumstances over which my concerns cast their shadow even as they were subtly altered in turn, much as an ancient monument and the dwellings of a later time built at its base reciprocally alter the appearance of one another. Of course, as I recall that journey, I do not place myself within the same viewpoints that my companions do, for it is summarized in a series of impressions known only to myself. Nor can it be said that through memory I place myself only in the viewpoint of my relatives, friends, and favorite authors. I traveled that mountainous route with companions of given character and looks, and I inattentively participated in their conversations while my thoughts ranged in a former milieu. All the while, the impressions flowing within me were like so many novel and particular ways of considering persons dear to me and the bonds uniting us. However, in their novelty, in the many elements not found in my previous thinking of my more intimate thoughts at the time, these impressions were in another sense alien to these groups as well. They express in this manner those groups closest to us only if the latter are not physically present. Probably everything I saw and everyone I listened to attracted my attention only to the extent they made me feel the absence of these groups. Don't we distinguish this viewpoint—which is neither that of our present companions nor purely and completely that of our friends of yesterday and tomorrow—in order to attribute it to ourself? Isn't the attractiveness of this impression in what is not explained by our relationships with either group, what contrasts sharply to their thought and experience? I know that it cannot be shared or even surmised by my companions. I also know that it could not have been suggested to me in its present form and framework by my relatives and friends, about whom I was thinking at the time and to whom I now return through memory. Therefore, is there not some residue of that impression that escapes both groups and exists only for me?

What stand in the foreground of group memory are remembrances of events and experiences of concern to the greatest number of members. These arise either out of group life itself or from relationships with the nearest and most frequently contacted groups. Remembrances concerning very few members (perhaps only one) merge into the background, even though they are included in the group memory, because they have at least partially occurred within group boundaries. Two people can feel very close and share all their thoughts. If they should later come to live in different milieus, they could, through letters when apart or conversation when together, make one another acquainted with the circumstances of their new lives. But they would still need to identify with one another if everything in their experiences foreign to the other were to be assimilated into their common thought. Mlle. de Lespinasse's letters could make the Comte de Guibert understand her feelings from afar. But she was active in the higher social circles and fashionable milieus with which membership made him also familiar. He could look at his lover, as she herself could, by putting himself within the viewpoint of these men and women who were completely unaware of their romance. He could also picture her, as she herself could, from the viewpoint of that closed and secret group that the two comprise. Unknown to him who is far away, however, many changes could occur in that society that her letters might not adequately document. He might never become aware of her changing attitude toward her social world. The fact that he loves her as he does would not suffice to divine these changes in her.

Ordinarily, a group has relationships with other groups. Many events derive from such contacts, and many conceptions have no other source. These contacts and relationships may be permanent, or at least repeated often enough to endure for a long period. For example, when a family lives for a long time in the same town or near the same friends, family and town or family and friends compose a sort of complex group. Remembrances arise that are included in the framework of thought of each group. An individual must belong to both groups to recognize a remembrance of this type. This condition is fulfilled by only a part of the membership of either group over any length of time, and even then in an incomplete way by family members whose main interest is their family. Moreover, family members who move, and are now influenced almost exclusively by family, lose their capacity to remember what they retained only because they were under the influence of two converging currents of collective thought. Furthermore, since only some members of each group are included in the other, both of these collective influences are weaker than if they acted alone. For example, only a portion of the family and not the whole group can help a member recall this particular set of memories. An individual will recall and recognize such remembrances only if placed in a situation permitting these two influences to best combine their action upon him. Consequently, the remembrance seems less familiar, easily hides the collective factors determining it, and gives the illusion of being less under voluntary control.

The Individual Remembrance as the Intersection of Collective Influences

Often we deem ourselves the originators of thoughts and ideas, feelings and passions, actually inspired by some group. Our agreement with those about us is so complete that we vibrate in unison, ignorant of the real source of the vibrations. How often do we present, as deeply held convictions, thoughts borrowed from a newspaper, book, or conversation? They respond so well to our way of seeing things that we are surprised to discover that their author is someone other than ourself. "That's just what I think about that!" We are unaware that we are but an echo. The whole art of the orator probably consists in his giving listeners the illusion that the convictions and feelings he arouses within them have come not from him but from themselves, that he has only divined and lent his voice to what has been worked out in their innermost consciousness. In one way or another, each social group endeavors to maintain a similar persuasion over its members. How many people are critical enough to discern what they owe to others in their thinking and so acknowledge to themselves how small their own contribution usually is? Occasionally an individual increases the range of his acquaintances and readings, making a virtue of an eclecticism that permits him to view and reconcile divergent aspects of things. Even in such instances the particular dosage of opinions, the complexity of feelings and desires, may only express his accidental relationships with groups divergent or opposed on some issue. The relative value attributed to each way of looking at things is really a function of the respective intensity of influences that each group has separately exerted upon him. In any case, insofar as we yield without struggle to an external suggestion, we believe we are free in our thought and feelings. Therefore most social influences we obey usually remain unperceived.

But this is probably even more true for these complex states that occur at the intersection of several currents of collective thought, states we are wont to see as unique events existing only for ourself. A traveler suddenly caught up by influences from a milieu foreign to his companions, a child exposed to adult feelings and concerns by unexpected circumstances, someone who has experienced a change of location, occupation, or family that hasn't totally ruptured his bonds with previous groups—all are instances of this phenomenon. Often the social influences concerned are much more complex, being more numerous and interwoven. Hence they are more difficult and more confusing to unravel. We see each milieu by the light of the other (or others) as well as its own and so gain an impression of resisting it. Certainly each of these influences ought to emerge more sharply from their comparison and contrast. Instead, the confrontation of these milieus gives us a feeling of no longer being involved in any of them. What becomes paramount is the "strangeness" of our situation, absorbing individual thought enough to screen off the social thoughts whose conjunction has elaborated it. This strangeness cannot be fully understood by any other member of these milieus, only myself. In this sense it belongs to me and, at the moment of its occurrence, I am tempted to explain it by reference to myself and myself alone. At the most, I might concede that circumstances (that is, the conjunction of these milieus) have served as the occasion permitting the production of an event long ago incorporated in my individual destiny, the appearance of a feeling latent in my innermost person. I have no other means of explaining its subsequent return to memory, because others were unaware of it and have had no role in its production (as we mistakenly imagine). Therefore, in one way or another, it must have been preserved in its original form in my mind. But that is not the case at all. These remembrances that seem purely personal, since we alone are aware of and capable of retrieving them, are distinguished by the greater complexity of the conditions necessary for their recall. But this is a difference in degree only.

One doctrine is satisfied to note that our past comprises two kinds of elements. Certain elements we can evoke whenever we want. By contrast, others cannot simply be summoned and we seem to encounter various obstacles in searching for them in our past. In reality, the first type might be said to belong to a common domain, in the sense that they are familiar or easily accessible to others as well as ourself. The idea we most easily picture to ourself, no matter how personal and specific its elements, is the idea others have of us. The events of our life most immediate to ourself are also engraved in the memory of those groups closest to us. Hence, facts and conceptions we possess with least effort are recalled to us from a common domain (common at least to one or several milieus). These remembrances are "everybody's" to this extent. We can recall them whenever we want just because we can base ourself on the memory of others. The second type, which cannot be recalled at will, are readily acknowledged to be available only to ourself because only we could have known about them. So we apparently end up in this strange paradox. The remembrances we evoke with most difficulty are our concern alone and constitute our most exclusive possession. They seem to escape the purview of others only at the expense of escaping ourself also. It is as if a person locked his treasure in a safe with a lock so complicated that he could not open it; he does not remember the combination and must rely on chance to remind him of it.

But there is an explanation at once simpler and more natural. The difference between remembrances we evoke at will and remembrances we seem to command no longer is merely a matter of degree of complexity. The former are always at hand because they are preserved in groups that we enter at will and collective thoughts to which we remain closely related. The elements of these remembrances and their relationships are all familiar to us. The latter are less accessible because the groups that carry them are more remote and intermittent in contact with us. Groups that associate frequently enable us to be in them simultaneously, whereas others have so little contact that we have neither intention nor occasion to trace their faded paths of communication. Now it is along such routes, along such sheltered pathways, that we retrieve those remembrances that are uniquely our own. In the same way, a traveler might consider as his own a spring, an outcropping of rock, or a landscape reached only by leaving the main thoroughfare and rejoining another via a rough and infrequently used trail. The starting points of such a short cut lie on the main routes and are common knowledge. But close scrutiny and maybe a bit of luck are required to find them again. A person might frequently pass by either without bothering to look for them, especially if he couldn't count upon passers-by to point them out, passers-by who travel one of these thoroughfares but have no concern to go where the other might lead.

Let us not hesitate to return to the examples we have discussed. We will clearly see that the "starting points," or the elements of these personal remembrances that seem to be uniquely our own, can easily be found preserved in definite social milieus. The members of these groups (we ourselves have not ceased to belong) know how to find and show them to us, if we only interrogate them in the appropriate manner. Our traveling companions did not know the relatives and friends we left behind. But they did observe that we never fully joined them. They sensed moments when we seemed more like a stranger. Were we to meet them later, they could recall our distracted manner or reflections and comments indicating that our thoughts were elsewhere. The child who was lost in the woods, or who confronted some dangerous situation that aroused in him feelings of an adult, told nothing of this to his parents. But they observed that afterward he was not so careless as he used to be (as if a shadow had been cast over him), and that on seeing them he displayed a joy no longer so childlike. The inhabitants of the town to which I moved did not know where I came from, but before I had become used to my new surroundings, my astonishment, curiosity, and ignorance had undoubtedly been noticed by some of the townspeople. These scarcely noticeable traces of events having little import for this new milieu probably attracted attention only for a short while. Nevertheless, were I to relate the events responsible for these traces, some would still remember those traces or at least know where to look.

While the collective memory endures and draws strength from its base in a coherent body of people, it is individuals as group members who remember. While these remembrances are mutually supportive of each other and common to all, individual members still vary in the intensity with which they experience them. I would readily acknowledge that each memory is a viewpoint on the collective memory, that this viewpoint changes as my position changes, that this position itself changes as my relationships to other milieus change. Therefore, it is not surprising that everyone does not draw on the same part of this common instrument. In accounting for that diversity, however, it is always necessary to revert to a combination of influences that are social in nature.

Certain of these combinations are extremely complex. Hence their appearance is not under our control. In a sense, we must trust to chance. We must wait for the various systems of waves (in those social milieus where we move mentally or physically) to intersect again and cause that registering apparatus which is our individual consciousness to vibrate the same way it did in the past. But the type of causality is the same and could not be different from what it was then. The succession of our remembrances, of even our most personal ones, is always explained by changes occurring in our relationships to various collective milieus—in short, by the transformations these milieus undergo separately and as a whole.

Some may say how strange it is that our most personal remembrances, offering such a striking character of absolute unity, actually derive from a fusion of diverse and separate elements. First of all, reflection shows this unity to dissolve rapidly into a multiplicity. It has been claimed that one recovers, when plumbing the depths of a truly personal conscious state, the whole content of mind as seen from a certain viewpoint. But "content of mind" must be understood as all the elements that mark its relationships to various milieus. A personal state thus reveals the complexity of the combination that was its source. Its apparent unity is explained by a quite natural type of illusion. Philosophers have shown that the feeling of liberty may be explained by the multiplicity of causal series that combine to produce an action. We conceive each influence as being opposed by some other and thus believe we act independently of each influence since we do not act under the exclusive power of any one. We do not perceive that our act really results from their action in concert, that our act is always governed by the law of causality. Similarly, since the remembrance reappears, owing to the interweaving of several series of collective thoughts, and since we cannot attribute it to any single one, we imagine it independent and contrast its unity to their multiplicity. We might as well assume that a heavy object, suspended in air by means of a number of very thin and interlaced wires, actually rests in the void where it holds itself up.

2. Historical Memory and Collective Memory

Autobiographical Memory and Historical Memory: Their Apparent Opposition

We are not accustomed to speaking, even metaphorically, of a "group memory." Such a faculty, it would seem, could exist and endure only insofar as it was bound to a person's body and brain. However, suppose that remembrances are organized in two ways, either grouped about a definite individual who considers them from his own viewpoint or distributed within a group for which each is a partial image. Then there is an "individual memory" and a "collective memory." In other words, the individual participates in two types of memory, but adopts a quite different, even contrary, attitude as he participates in the one or the other. On the one hand, he places his own remembrances within the framework of his personality, his own personal life; he considers those of his own that he holds in common with other people only in the aspect that interests him by virtue of distinguishing him from others. On the other hand, he is able to act merely as a group member, helping to evoke and maintain impersonal remembrances of interest to the group. These two memories are often intermingled. In particular, the individual memory, in order to corroborate and make precise and even to cover

50

the gaps in its remembrances, relies upon, relocates itself within, momentarily merges with, the collective memory. Nonetheless, it still goes its own way, gradually assimilating any acquired deposits. The collective memory, for its part, encompasses the individual memories while remaining distinct from them. It evolves according to its own laws, and any individual remembrances that may penetrate are transformed within a totality having no personal consciousness.

Let us now examine the individual memory. It is not completely sealed off and isolated. A man must often appeal to others' remembrances to evoke his own past. He goes back to reference points determined by society, hence outside himself. Moreover, the individual memory could not function without words and ideas, instruments the individual has not himself invented but appropriated from his milieu. Nevertheless, it is true that one remembers only what he himself has seen, done, felt, and thought at some time. That is, our own memory is never confused with anyone else's. Both the individual memory and the collective memory have rather limited, but differing, spatial and temporal boundaries. Those of the collective memory may be either more compressed or more extended.

During my life, my national society has been theater for a number of events that I say I "remember," events that I know about only from newspapers or the testimony of those directly involved. These events occupy a place in the memory of the nation, but I myself did not witness them. In recalling them, I must rely entirely upon the memory of others, a memory that comes, not as corroborator or completer of my own, but as the very source of what I wish to repeat. I often know such events no better nor in any other manner than I know historical events that occurred before I was born. I carry a baggage load of historical remembrances that I can increase through conversation and reading. But it remains a borrowed memory, not my own. These events have deeply influenced national thought, not only because they have altered institutions but also because their tradition endures, very much alive, in region, province, political party, occupation, class, even certain families or persons who experienced them firsthand. For me they are conceptions, symbols. I picture them pretty much as others do. I can imagine them, but I cannot remember them. I belong to a group with a part of my personality, so that everything that has occurred within it as long as I belonged—even everything that interested and transformed it before I entered—is in some sense familiar to me. But should I wish to restore the remembrance of a certain event in its entirety, I would have to bring together all the partial and distorted reproductions concerning it that are held by all group members. By contrast, my personal remembrances are wholly mine, wholly in me.

Therefore, there is reason to distinguish two sorts of memory. They might be labeled, if one prefers, internal or inward memory and external memory, or personal memory and social memory. I would consider more accurate "autobiographical memory" and "historical memory." The former would make use of the latter, since our life history belongs, after all, to general history. Naturally, historical memory would cover a much broader expanse of time. However, it would represent the past only in a condensed and schematic way, while the memory of our own life would present a richer portrait with greater continuity.

If our personal memory is understood to be something that we know only from within, while the collective memory would be known only from without, then the two will surely contrast sharply. I remember Reims because I lived there a whole year. But I also remember that Joan of Arc consecrated Charles VII there, because I have heard it said or read it. The story of Joan of Arc has been presented so often on the stage, on the movie screen, or elsewhere that I truly have no difficulty imagining Joan of Arc at Reims. Meanwhile, I certainly know that I was not a witness to the event itself, that I cannot go beyond these words heard or read by me, that these symbols passed down through time are all that comes to me from that past. The same is true for every historical fact I know. Proper names, dates, formulas summarizing a long sequence of details, occasional anecdotes or quotations, are the epitaphs to those bygone events, as brief, general, and scant of meaning as most tombstone inscriptions. History indeed resembles a crowded cemetery, where room must constantly be made for new tombstones.

Were the past social milieu to live for us only in these historical notations, and, more generally speaking, were the collective memory composed only of dates, arbitrary definitions, and reminders of events, then it would most assuredly remain external to us. Many citizens of our vast national societies never participate in the common interests of the majority, who read the newspaper and pay some attention to public affairs. Even we who do not so isolate ourselves may periodically become so absorbed that we no longer follow "current events." Later on, we may find ourselves reassembling around such a period in our life the public events of that time. For example, what happened in France and the world in 1877, the year I was born? It was the year of the "16th of May," when the volatile political situation truly gave birth to the Third Republic. DeBroglie was in power, and Gambetta declared that "he must resign or be forcibly removed." The painter Courbet died. Victor Hugo published the second volume of *Legende des Siècles*. The Boulevard Saint-Germain was completed in Paris, and construction began on the Avenue de la République. The attention of all Europe focused on Russia's war against Turkey. Osman Pasha was forced to surrender Plevna after a long and heroic defense. I thus reconstitute a rather spacious framework, in which I feel myself quite lost. I am doubtless caught up in the current of national life, but I hardly feel involved. I am like a passenger on a boat. As the riverbanks pass by, everything he sees is neatly fitted into the total landscape. But suppose he loses himself in thought or is distracted by his traveling companions; he concerns himself only occasionally with what passes along the banks. Later on, he will be able to remember where he has traveled but few details of the landscape, and he will be able to trace his route on a map. Such a traveler may recover some forgotten memories or make others more precise, but he has not really had contact with the country through which he passed.

Certain psychologists apparently prefer to imagine historical events as auxiliary to our memory, functioning much as do the temporal partitions of a watch or calendar. Our life flows by in a continuous movement. But when we look back at what has unrolled, we always find it possible to assign its various portions to the demarcations of collective time. Such temporal divisions are imposed from outside upon every individual memory precisely because their source is not in any single one of them. A social time defined in this way would truly be external to the lived duration of each consciousness. We see this clearly in the case of a watch measuring astronomical time. But the same is also true of those dates on the clock-face of history: they correspond to the most noteworthy events of national life, the occurrence of which we may be unaware of, the importance of which we recognize only later. Our lives thus sit on the surface of social bodies, merely observing their alterations and putting up with their disturbances. An event takes its place in the sequence of historical facts only some time after its occurrence. Thus we can link the various phases of our life to national events only after the fact. Nothing demonstrates better how artificial and external is that operation that consists of referring to demarcations of collective life for mental landmarks. Nothing demonstrates more clearly that we really study distinct objects when we focus on either individual memory or collective memory. The events and dates constituting the very substance of group life can be for the individual only so many external signs, which he can use as reference points only by going outside himself.

Of course, the collective memory would play a very secondary role in the fixation of our remembrances if it had no other content than such sequences of dates or lists of facts. But such a conception is remarkably narrow and does not correspond to reality. For that very reason I have had difficulty presenting it in this way. However, such an approach was necessary, for this conception accords with a widely accepted doctrine. The memory is usually considered as a properly individual faculty—that is, as appearing in a consciousness reduced solely to its own resources, isolated from anyone else and capable of evoking by will or chance states previously experienced. Nevertheless, since it is impossible to deny that we often replace our remembrances within a space and time whose demarcations we share with others, or that we also situate them within dates that have meaning only in relation to a group to which we belong, these facts are acknowledged to be the case. But it is a sort of minimal concession that does not impair, in the minds of those granting it, the specificity of the individual memory.

The Real Interpenetration of Historical and Autobiographical Memory (Contemporary History)

As Stendhal observed:

Now as I write my life in 1835, I make many discoveries. . . . They are like great fragments of fresco on a wall, which, long forgotten, reappear suddenly, and by the side of these well-preserved fragments there are . . . great gaps where there's nothing to be seen but the bricks of the wall. The plaster on which the fresco had been painted has fallen and the fresco has gone forever. There are no dates besides the pieces of fresco that remain, and now in 1835, I have to hunt for the dates. Fortunately there's no harm in an anachronism, a confusion of a year or two. After my arrival in Paris in 1799, my life became involved with public events and all dates are certain. . . . In 1835, I discover the shape and the "why" of past events.[1]

Such dates and the historical and national events they represent (for this is surely the sense in which Stendahl understands them) can be totally external, at least in appearance, to the circumstances of our life. But later on, as we reflect upon them, we "make many discoveries"; we "discover the shape and the 'why' of events." This might be understood in various ways. When I page through a contemporary history and review the sequence of events in France or Europe since my birth, during the first eight or ten years of my life, I indeed get the impression of an external framework of which I was then unaware and I learn to relocate my childhood within the history of my times. Even though I clarify from outside this first period of my life, however, my memory scarcely grows richer in its personal aspect. I gain no revelations of my childhood; nothing new

[1] Stendhal, *Vie d'Henri Brulard*, ed. Henri Martineau (Paris: Le Divan I, 1949), p. 151.

emerges. I did not yet read newspapers or participate in adult conversation. At present I can formulate an idea, necessarily arbitrary, of the national affairs that were of lasting interest to my parents, but I have no direct remembrances of these events or my parents' reactions to them. It seems clear to me that the first national event that penetrated the fabric of my childhood impressions was the funeral of Victor Hugo. (I was then eight years old.) I see myself at my father's side, walking towards the Arc de Triomphe de l'Etoile where the catafalque had been erected; I see myself the next day watching the funeral parade from a balcony at the corner of the Rue Soufflot and the Rue Gay-Lussac.

Had nothing, then, of my encompassing national group filtered down to me and my narrow circle of concerns until this time? Yet I was always with my parents. They were exposed to many influences. They were, in part, the people they were because they lived through that period, in a certain country under certain national and political circumstances. Perhaps I can find no trace of definite "historical" events in their overt habits, in the general tone of their feelings. But there certainly existed in France during the ten-, fifteen-, or twenty-year period following the Franco-Prussian War of 1870–1871 a remarkable psychological and social atmosphere unique to this time. My parents belonged to this period; they acquired certain habits and characteristics that became part of their personality and made an early impression upon me. What is at issue here is no longer mere dates or facts. Of course, even contemporary history too often boils down to a series of overly abstract conceptions. But I can fill in these conceptions, substituting images and impressions for these ideas, when I look over the paintings, portraits, and engravings of the time or think about the books that appeared, the plays presented, the style of the period, the jokes and humor in vogue.

I don't fancy that this picture of a world so recently vanished and now re-created by artificial means will become the slightly contrived background on which to project profiles of my parents—a sort of solution in which I immerse my own past in order to "develop" it, as one might a film. On the contrary, the world of my childhood, as I recover it from memory, fits so naturally into the framework of recent history reconstituted by formal study because it already bears the stamp of that history. What I discover is that by attentive effort I can recover, in my remembrances of my little world, a semblance of the surrounding social milieu. Many scattered details, perhaps too familiar for me to have ever considered connecting them and inquiring into their meaning, now stand out and come together. I learn to distinguish, in the character of my parents and the period, what can be accounted for not by human nature or circumstances common to other periods but only by the peculiarities of the national milieu at that time. My parents—indeed their friends and every adult I met then—were (like all of us) a product of their times. When I want to picture that period's life and thought, I direct my reflections toward them. This is what makes contemporary history interest me in a way the history of preceding periods cannot. Of course, I cannot claim to remember the particulars of these events, since I am familiar with them only through reading. But, in contrast to other periods, the time contemporary with my childhood lives in my memory because I was immersed within it and one facet of my remembrances is but a reflection of it.

Even when considering childhood remembrances, then, we are better off not to distinguish a personal memory that would reproduce past impressions just as they originally were and would never take us beyond the restricted circle of our family, school, and friends, from a "historical" memory that would be composed only of national events unfamiliar to us as children. We had best avoid this distinction between one memory that puts us in touch with only ourself (or with a self, really, broadened to include the group encompassing the world of the child) and another memory that enables us to penetrate into a milieu of which we were unaware at the time but within which our life actually unfolded. Our memory truly rests not on learned history but on lived history. By the term "history" we must understand, then, not a chronological sequence of events and dates, but whatever distinguishes one period from all others, something of which books and narratives generally give us only a very schematic and incomplete picture.

I will probably be accused of stripping from this form of collective memory we call "history" its impersonal character, this abstract precision and relative simplicity that makes so appropriate a framework to bolster our individual memory. If we limit ourselves to the impressions made on us by such events in history, or by our parents' attitudes toward events that later on gain historical significance, or even by the customs, the ways of speaking and acting peculiar to a period, what would distinguish these from anything else that concerned our childhood but was not retained in the national memory? How could the child evaluate the successive portions of the picture life unfolds before him? Above all, why should he be attracted by the facts and characteristics of interest to adults, especially as he lacks the many spatial and temporal terms for comparison that adults possess?

In effect, a war, rebellion, national ceremony, popular festivity, new kind of transportation, or great construction can be considered from two distinct viewpoints. They are events, unique in their kind, that alter group life. But they also dissolve into a series of images traversing the individual consciousness. The child retaining only these images would find that some stand out in his mind due to their brilliance, intensity, and unique quality. The same would occur for many images of lesser events. Imagine a child arriving at night at a railroad station crowded with soldiers. Whether they were on their way to, or back from, the trenches, or merely on maneuvers, would make no difference at all to him. Wouldn't the distant artillery of Waterloo be but muted thunder? Any being resembling such a youngster, reduced solely to his perceptions, would keep only a fragile and transitory remembrance of such a scene. To grasp the historical reality underlying that image, he would have to go outside himself and be placed within a group viewpoint, so that he might see how such an event marked a famous date because it is imbued with the concerns, interests, passions, of a nation. But at that moment the event would cease to be merely a personal impression. We have regained contact with the scheme of history. Thus my critic would conclude that the individual must rely on the historical memory. Through it, a fact external to my childhood stamps its mark on a certain hour or day and enables me to recall those moments later on. But the mark itself is a superficial stamping from outside, unconnected with my personal memory or childhood impressions.

Underlying such an analysis, however, remains the idea that minds are as neatly compartmentalized as the organisms physically supporting them. Each of us is first and foremost sealed within himself. How to account, then, for the fact that one person communicates and adapts his thoughts to those of others? My critic might admit that the individual creates some kind of artificial milieu, external to every one of these personal thoughts, though encompassing them all—a collective space and time, a collective history. The thoughts of all persons come together within such frameworks, which assume that each has momentarily ceased to be himself. Each person soon returns into himself, introducing into his memory the ready-made reference points and demarcations brought from without. We connect our remembrances to these reference points, without any sharing of substance or closer relationship occurring between them. That is why these general and historical conceptions play only a secondary role: they actually presuppose the prior and autonomous existence of the personal memory. Collective remembrances might be laid on individual remembrances, providing a handier and surer grip on them. First, however, individual remembrances must be present, lest memory function without content. Surely there must have been a day when I met a certain friend for the first time or, as Blondel says, when I attended the *lycée* for the first time.[2] These are historical conceptions. But if I haven't inwardly preserved a personal remembrance of that first meeting or first day of class, this conception would remain up in the air, that framework would be empty, and I would recall nothing—so obvious does it seem that there is in every act of memory an element specific to it, that is the very existence of self-sufficient individual consciousness.

[2] Charles Blondel, "Critical Review of Maurice Halbwachs' *Les Cadres sociaux de la mémoire*," *Revue philosophique 101* (1926), p. 296.

Lived History in Childhood

But such a distinction—between a memory employing no frameworks, or at best only words and a few conceptions borrowed from practical life, to order its remembrances, and a collective or historical framework without any memory, because it is never constructed, reconstructed, and preserved in the memory of the individual—is not very plausible. As soon as a child leaves the stage of purely sensory life and becomes interested in the meaning of images and scenes that he perceives, it can be said that he thinks in common with others, that his thought is divided between the flood of wholly personal impressions and the various currents of collective thought. He is no longer enclosed within himself, for his thinking now commands entirely new perspectives which he knows are not his alone. Nor has he gone outside himself and perforce compartmentalized his mind to accommodate these series of thoughts common in his group, because these new outwardly oriented concerns have always interested the "inner man" in one way or another and are not entirely foreign to his personal life.

From the balcony of his grandfather's home in Grenoble, Stendhal as a child witnessed the Day of the Tiles, a mass uprising at the start of the French Revolution.

Some forty-three years later, the image is as clear as ever in my mind. A journeyman hatter, stabbed in the back by a bayonet, so I heard, was walking in great pain supported by two men over whose shoulders his arms were laid. He wore no coat, his shirt and buff or white pants were soaked with blood. I can still see him. The wound from which the blood was pouring out was in the small of his back, about opposite the navel.

They were helping him to walk with great difficulty to his room on the sixth floor of the Périer house. He died on reaching it. . . .

I saw the poor wretch on each landing of the Périers' staircase, which was lighted by big windows overlooking the square.

This memory, naturally, is the clearest I have from those days.[3]

[3] *Vie d'Henri Brulard*, p. 121.

This is an image all right, but an image centered within a scene of a mass revolution that Stendhal himself witnessed. How often must he have heard that story told later on, especially since this uprising apparently initiated a turbulent and decisive period in politics. In any case, even were he unaware of the place this day would have in history (at least in Grenoble's history), he could surmise from the extraordinary activity in the street, and from the gestures and comments of his relatives, that this event went beyond the circle of family and neighborhood. Another day during this period, he sees himself in the library, listening to his grandfather, who is in a room full of people. "But why such a crowd? What was the occasion? The image does not tell me that. It's no more than an image." Nonetheless, would he have preserved such a remembrance (as he did of the Day of Tiles) were it not fitted within a framework of enduring concerns that emerged within him at this time, concerns that already involved him in a more extensive current of collective thought?

The remembrance may not be immediately caught up in such a current, and some time may elapse before the meaning of the event is understood. What is essential is that the meaning should soon become clear, while the remembrance is still fresh. Then we see radiating from and about the remembrance its historical significance, as it were. The attitude of adults who are also present confirms that an event that has attracted our notice merits retention. We remember it because others about us are interested in it. Later on we will better understand why. Caught at first within the main current, perhaps the remembrance had been sidetracked by the greenery along the riverbank. Currents of collective thought flow through the child's mind, but only in the long run do they gather in everything belonging to them.

One of my earliest remembrances is of a small hotel where Russians stayed. It was located opposite our house on Rue Gay-Lussac, next to a convent, on the present site of the oceanographic institute. I remember them in their fur caps, sitting by the door with their wives and children. Despite their strange features and dress, I might not have watched them so much had not passers-by stopped, and my own parents come out on the balcony to look at them. Bitten by rabid wolves, these inhabitants of Siberia settled in Paris near the Rue d'Ulm and the École Normale to receive treatment from Pasteur. For the first time I heard that name and pictured to myself the existence of scientists who make discoveries. I have no idea how much I understood of such matters. Perhaps I fully understood it only later. But I do not believe that this remembrance would have remained so clear in my mind had not this image oriented my thought to new horizons, toward unknown regions from which I felt gradually less distant.

Such disturbances of a social milieu, which cause the child to suddenly get a glimpse of the political and national life beyond his own narrow circle, are infrequent. When he finally joins serious adult conversation or reads the newspapers, the child will feel himself discovering an unknown land. But this will not be the first time that he has come in contact with a social milieu more extensive than his family or his small circle of playmates and parents' friends. Parents and children each have their own interests. The boundaries separating these two zones of thought are, for many reasons, not surmounted. But the child does come in contact with a class of adults whose level of thought approximates his own—servants, for example. The child readily converses with them, taking revenge against the silence and reserve to which his parents condemn him in matters that he is "too young" to know about. Servants may talk freely to and with the child, who understands because they often communicate in a childlike manner. Almost all that I learned and could understand of the Franco-Prussian War, Paris Commune, Second Empire, and Third Republic came from a good old woman, full of superstition and prejudice, who blindly accepted the picture of events and regimes painted by popular imagination. She informed me of the vague rumors that like the backwash of history, spread among the peasants, workers, and common people. My parents could only shake their heads in disbelief at hearing such tales. In those moments I gained an understanding, however confused, of the human milieus disturbed by these events, if not of the events themselves. Even today my memory evokes that first historical framework of childhood along with my earliest impressions. In any case, this was the way I first pictured events just before my birth. If I now recognize how inaccurate these stories really were, I can only affirm that I took a sympathetic interest in those troubled waters and that more than one of those confused images still managed to enframe, even as it deformed, some of my remembrances from that time.

The Living Bond of Generations

The child is provided access to an even more distant past by his grandparents. Perhaps grandparents and grandchildren become close because both are, for different reasons, uninterested in the contemporary events that engross the parents. As Marc Bloch says:

> In rural societies, the young are quite frequently left entrusted during the day to the care of the "old." The father is occupied in the field and the mother is preoccupied with the many household tasks. The child receives as much, and even more, of the legacy of various customs and traditions from them as from his parents.[4]

The grandparents and the elderly are clearly products of their own times. The child doesn't immediately perceive and distinguish those characteristics in his grandfather due solely to age from those stamped on him by that society, now extinct, in which he lived and grew up. The child, on arriving in the city, neighborhood, and home of his grandfather, vaguely senses that he is entering a different territory. It is not foreign to him, however, for it agrees very well with the character of the oldest members of his family. He is aware that, for his grandparents, he somewhat replaces his parents, who should have remained children and not become totally involved in contemporary life and society. Their stories, oblivious of the times and linking the past and future together across the present, could not help but intrigue him, just as stories about himself might.

[4] Marc Bloch, "Mémoire collective, traditions et coutumes," *Revue de synthèse historique*, Nos. 118–120 (1925), p. 79.

What becomes fixed in his memory are not just facts, but attitudes and ways of thinking from the past. We may regret having not taken fuller advantage of this unique opportunity to gain direct contact with a period that we would otherwise have known only from outside, through history books, paintings, and literature. Be that as it may, the personage of an aged relative seems to grow in our memory as we are told of a past time and society; instead of remaining a shadowy figure, he then emerges with all the clarity and color of a person who is the center of a portrait and who sums up and epitomizes it.

Of all his family, why did Stendhal happen to remember his grandfather so clearly and to sketch his portrait so vividly? Didn't Stendhal see him as personifying the end of the eighteenth century? The grandfather had known some of the *philosophes* and had helped him to truly comprehend that pre-Revolutionary society for which Stendhal never lost his fondness. If Stendhal had not linked in his earliest thoughts the person of that old man with the works of Diderot, Voltaire, and d'Alembert and a whole body of interests and feelings transcending the restricted and conservative boundaries of a small province, then the grandfather would have never been, for Stendhal, the esteemed and oft quoted relative that he was. Perhaps he would have been remembered with equal accuracy, but he certainly would not have occupied so important a place in the writer's memory. It is that "lived" eighteenth century suffusing his thought that restores to Stendhal the in-depth likeness of his grandfather. Collective frameworks of memory do not amount to so many names, dates, and formulas, but truly represent currents of thought and experience within which we recover our past only because we have lived it.

History is neither the whole nor even all that remains of the past. In addition to written history, there is a living history that perpetuates and renews itself through time and permits the recovery of many old currents that have seemingly disappeared. If this were not so, what right would we have to speak of a "collective memory"? What service could possibly be rendered by frameworks that have endured only as so many desiccated and impersonal historical conceptions? Groups that develop the reigning conceptions and mentality of a society during a certain period fade away in time, making room for others, who in turn command the sway of custom and fashion opinion from new models. The world we shared so deeply with our grandparents may have suddenly vanished. We may have very few extrafamilial remembrances of that intermediate period between the older world before our birth and the contemporary national period that so engrosses us. It is as if, during an intermission, the old people's world faded away and the stage were filled with new characters. Nonetheless, let us see if we cannot find a milieu, a state of past thought and sensibility, that has left all the traces necessary for its provisional recreation.

Many times I have thought that I perceived, in that group composed of my grandparents and myself, the last reverberations of romanticism. By "romanticism" I mean a particular type of sensibility, not identical with that of the figures included in the late-eighteenth-century artistic and literary movement so named, though no longer clearly distinguished from it either. Though somewhat dissipated in the frivolities of the Second Empire, it held on tenaciously in the more remote provinces (and it is there, indeed, that I have rediscovered its last vestiges). It is quite legitimate to try to reconstruct this milieu, to reconstitute that atmosphere about ourselves through books, engravings, and paintings. Our primary concern is not with the great poets and their work. In fact, their writings affect us in ways quite different from those in which they affected contemporaries. We have made many discoveries about them. Rather, this mentality, which permeated everything and showed itself in multifarious ways, is locked up as it were in the magazines and "family literature" of the time. As we page through such publications, we seem to see the old folks once again, with the gestures, expressions, poses, and dress of period engravings; we seem to hear their voices and recognize the very expressions they used. Of course, these "family museums" and popular magazines are accidental leftovers to which we might never have had access. Nonetheless, if I do reopen these books, or if I do rediscover these engravings, pictures, and portraits, I am not driven by scholarly curiosity and love of what is old to consult them in a library or view them in a museum. I discover them in my own home, in my parents' and friends' homes, on the wharves, and in the windows of antique shops.

In addition to engravings and books, the past has left many other traces, occasionally visible, in present-day society. We see it in people's appearance, the look of a place, and even in the unconscious ways of thinking and feeling preserved by certain persons and milieus. Ordinarily we don't notice such things. But we need alter our attention only slightly to see the outcroppings of the older strata underlying modern customs.

We may have to go some distance to discover those islands of the past so genuine in their preservation as to make us feel as though we have suddenly been carried back fifty or sixty years. One day in Vienna, I was invited to visit the family of a banker. In their home I had the feeling of being in a French salon of the 1830s. It was not so much the furniture or décor as the quite singular social atmosphere—an intangible something of the conventional and formal, like a glimmer from the *ancien régime*. On another occasion, I arrived in a part of Algeria where the Europeans lived some distance from each other. Forced to travel by stagecoach, I observed with curiosity men and women who seemed familiar, who resembled the people on engravings from the Second Empire. I conjectured that the French citizens who had come to settle this remote and isolated area after the conquest, and their descendants, had to live on a fund of ideas and customs dating from that period. In any case, each of these images (whether real or imaginary) became connected in my mind with remembrances from similar milieus, in the one case, of an aged aunt sitting in such a salon and, in the other case, of a retired officer who had lived in Algeria during colonization. We can easily make similar observations without ever leaving France, Paris, or even our home town. Our urban areas have been transformed in the last fifty years. But there is more than one district in Paris, more than one street or block of homes, that contrasts sharply to the rest of the city and preserves its original appearance. Moreover, the residents resemble the locale. Indeed, in every period there is an intimate relationship between the habits and mentality of a group and the appearance of its residential areas. There was a Paris of 1860, with an image closely bound to the society and customs of its time. To evoke it we must do more than search out the plaques commemorating the homes where its famous personages lived and died or read a history of the city. An observer will note many features of the past in the city and people of today, especially in those areas that have become havens for the crafts and, during certain holidays, in the small shop and working class areas of Paris (which have changed less than the rest of the city). But the Paris of bygone days is perhaps best recognized in the very small provincial cities. Here the types of people, even the dress and speech patterns, once encountered on Rue Saint-Honoré and the great promenades of Balzac's Paris have not yet disappeared.

Our grandparents leave their stamp on our parents. We were not aware of it in the past because we were much more sensitive then to what distinguished generations. Our parents marched in front of us and guided us into the future. The moment comes when they stop and we pass them by. Then we must turn back to see them, and now they seem in the grip of the past and woven into the shadows of bygone times. In a few deeply moving pages Marcel Proust describes how, in the weeks following his grandmother's death, his mother suddenly seemed to him to become identified with the deceased's traits, expression, and overall appearance. She acquired the image of the grandmother, as if the same type of person were reproduced in two successive generations. Is this merely a physiological change? If we recognize our grandparents in our parents, is it because our parents are growing old and quickly fill the empty places in the sequence of generations? Rather, it may be because our attention has changed focus. Our parents and grandparents represent for us two distinct and clearly separated periods. We do not perceive that our grandparents were more closely associated with the present, our parents with the past, than we imagined.

I became aware of the world about a decade after the Franco-Prussian War (1870). The Second Empire was a distant period corresponding to a society almost extinct. Now twelve to fifteen years separate me from the Great War. I suppose that, for my children, the pre-1914 society of which they know nothing recedes similarly into a past not reached by their memory. But, for me, there is no break in continuity between these two periods. I see the same society, doubtless changed by new experiences, relieved of older prejudices and concerns, enriched with novel elements, but still the same. Of course, there is a larger or smaller portion of illusion in my views as well as in my children's. A time will come when, looking about me, I will recognize only very few who lived and thought as I did before the War. A time will come when I will understand, as I have sometimes uneasily, that new generations have pushed ahead of my own, that a society whose aspirations and customs are quite foreign to me has taken the place of the one to which I was most intimately attached. And my children, having changed point of view, will be astonished to suddenly discover that I am so distant from them and so close to my parents in interests, ideas, memories. They and I will then be, doubtless, under the influence of a converse illusion: I am really not so distant from them because my parents were not really so distant from me. Depending on age and also circumstance, however, we are especially struck either by the differences between generations, as each retires into its own shell and grows distant from the other, or by the similarities, as they come together again and become as one.

Reconstructed Remembrances

To a much greater extent than is commonly believed, therefore, the life of the child is immersed in social milieus through which he comes in touch with a past stretching back some distance. The latter acts like a framework into which are woven his most personal remembrances. This is what I have endeavored to show in the previous analysis. Later on, his memory will ground itself on this lived past, much more than on any past learned from written history. Although at first he may not distinguish this framework from the conscious states placed within it, he gradually effects a separation between his little inner world and the surrounding society. Since both sorts of elements were intertwined from the beginning and seemed to comprise part of his childhood self, the most that can be said is that every element answering to the social milieu may later come forth as an abstract and artificial framework. In this sense lived history is clearly differentiated from written history: it possesses everything needed to constitute a living and natural framework upon which our thought can base itself to preserve and recover the image of its past.

But I must now pursue this further. As the child grows, and especially as he becomes an adult, he participates (at first unawares) in a more distinctive and reflective way in the life and thoughts of the groups to which he belongs. How could he help changing this idea of his past? How could his newly acquired conceptions—conceptions of facts, reflections and ideas—help reacting on his remembrances? As I have said many times, a remembrance is in very large measure a reconstruction of the past achieved with data borrowed from the present, a reconstruction prepared, furthermore, by reconstructions of earlier periods wherein past images had already been altered. Of course, if we presume memory to be a resumption of direct contact with certain past impressions, then a remembrance would, by definition, be distinguished from these ideas of varying precision whereby our reflections, assisted by others' stories, admissions, and evidence, make a determination of what our past must have been. Even were it possible to evoke directly a few remembrances, we could not distinguish such cases from those in which we imagine what happened. Hence we can consider remembrances as so many representations resting, at least in part, on testimony and reasoning. But the social or, if you prefer, "historical" facet of our memory of our own past is then much more extensive than we think. Having been in contact with adults since childhood, we have acquired quite a few means of retrieving and making precise our many remembrances that otherwise would have been partially or totally forgotten.

At this point we are faced with a previously noted objection that merits further examination. Can we restore entirely a remembrance of an event that did occur, but of which we have kept no impressions, merely by reconstructing a historical conception of it? For instance, I know with certainty, from reflection and from what I have been told, that there was a day when I attended the *lycée* for the first time. Nonetheless, I have no personal and direct remembrance of that event. My remembrances have become confused because of my having spent so many days there. Perhaps due to the excitement of the first day, "I have not memory of periods or moments when I felt too strongly," as Stendhal says in his autobiographical *Life of Henri Brulard*. Having restored the historical framework of that event, does it suffice for me to say that I have recreated a remembrance of it?

Of course, had I absolutely no remembrance of that event, had I to rely totally on a historical conception of it, then it could be concluded that an empty framework can never fill itself out all alone. It would be abstract knowledge at work, and not the memory. But, without actually remembering a given day, one can recall a certain period. Nor is it quite accurate to say that the remembrance of a period is simply the sum of the remembrances from each day. As events grow distant, we have a habit of recalling them in organized sets. Although certain remembrances may stand out clearly, many kinds of elements are included and we can neither enumerate each nor distinguish them from one another. Having successively attended primary schools, private boarding schools, and *lycées*, and being each year in a new class, I have a general remembrance of all these opening days of class that includes that particular day I first entered a *lycée*. Therefore I cannot say that I remember that specific return to school, but neither can I say that I no longer remember it. Moreover, a historical conception of my entrance into the *lycée* is not abstract. First of all, I have since read a number of factual and fictional accounts describing impressions of a child who is entering a class for the first time. It may very well be that, when I read them, the personal remembrance that I had kept of similar impressions became intertwined with the book's description. I can recall these narratives. Perhaps in time I have preserved and can retrieve, without being certain as to what is what, my own transposed impressions.

Whatever it may be, an idea thus "filled out" is no longer a mere schema without content. Let me add that I know and can retrieve a good deal more of that first *lycée* I attended than merely the school's name or map location. I was there each day during that time and have since returned several times. Even had I not visited it again as an adult, I am acquainted with *lycées* that my children have attended. I recall many features of that family milieu that I left on going to class, not because I remained in contact with a family in general but because I remained in touch with my family, a living and concrete group entering quite naturally into the picture I recreate of my first day of class. What objection can be raised, therefore, to the fact that I manage to recreate the general atmosphere and character of my first day of class by reflecting on what it must have been like? It is doubtless an incomplete and wavering image and certainly a reconstructed one. But how many of the remembrances that we believe genuine, with an identity beyond doubt, are almost entirely forged from false recognitions, in accordance with others' testimony and stories! A framework cannot produce of itself a precise and picturesque remembrance. But, in this case, the framework has been buoyed up with personal reflection and family remembrances: the remembrance is an image entangled among other images, a generic image taken back into the past.

Shrouded Remembrances

If I want to reassemble and make precise remembrances that would enable me to restore the look and character of my father as I knew him, I would likewise say that it would be quite useless to review the historical events of the period in which he lived. Nevertheless, if I meet an old acquaintance of his who gives me details and circumstances of his life of which I was unaware, or if my mother enlarges upon and fills in the picture of his life, clarifying portions that were obscure to me, do I not now have an impression of descending back into the past and augmenting a whole body of remembrances? We are not dealing in this case with a simple retrospective illusion. It is not as though I had rediscovered a letter of his that I read when he was alive, and that these new remembrances, owing to recent impressions, become juxtaposed to the original remembrances without becoming confused with them. Rather, the remembrance of my father as a whole is transformed and now seems to me to conform more to reality. The image I have of my father continuously evolved over time, not only because my remembrances of him while he lived accumulated but also because I myself changed and my perspective altered as I occupied different positions in my family and, more important, in other milieus. Nevertheless, will it be said that there is one image of my father that must take precedence over every other—namely, the image of him that was fixed at death? But how many times had it already been transformed before this moment? Besides, death may end physiological life, but it does not abruptly halt the current of thoughts unfolding in the social circles of the person whose body has been buried. For some time after, he will be considered as still alive and remain a part of daily life, as we imagine what he would have said or done in various situations. It is on the day after death that those closest to him focus most intensely on his person. At this time also, his image is least fixed and is continually transformed depending on the part of his life evoked. In reality, the image of a departed one is never frozen. As it recedes into the past, the image changes as certain features are effaced and others accentuated according to the perspective from which he is viewed—that is, depending on the new conditions in which we turn our attention upon him. I am inclined to retouch his portrait as I learn new things about my father from those variously connected with him, as I pass new judgment on the period in which he lived, and as I become more capable of reflection and possessed of more terms for comparison. Thus the past as I once knew it is slowly defaced. New images overlay the old—just as relatives closer in time are interposed between ourselves and our more distant ancestors—so that we know of the former only what the latter tell us. The groups to which I belong vary at different periods of my life. But it is from their viewpoint that I consider the past. As I become more involved in each of these groups and participate more intimately in its memory, I necessarily renovate and supplement my remembrances.

Of course, all this presupposes two conditions. First, my remembrances, before I entered these groups, were not fully clarified in all aspects; until now, so to speak, I did not fully perceive or understand them. Second, remembrances of these groups must have some connection with the events constituting my own past.

The first condition is satisfied by the fact that many of our remembrances date back to times when immaturity, inexperience, and inattention obscured the meaning of various facts or hid the nature of different persons or objects. We remained, as it were, overly concerned with the children's group even as we had become partially and loosely attached to the adult group. The result was a sort of chiaroscuro effect in the mind. What interested adults fascinated us also, only because we felt the adults were interested; and it remained in our memory as so many puzzles or problems that we did not yet understand but felt we could eventually solve. We may not even have noticed these unsettled aspects and zones of obscurity, but we did not forget them either, for they both surrounded and helped us to pass among our clearer remembrances. When a child falls asleep in his own bed only to awake aboard a train, he finds security in feeling that he remains under the watchful care of his parents in either place, even though he cannot understand how or why they have done what they have when he was asleep. There are many degrees of such ignorance. In one sense or another, we neither attain total clarity nor remain totally in the dark.

We may be able to picture some episode from our past not needing addition, correction, or further clarification. But then we may meet someone else who witnessed or participated in that event. As he recalls and recounts it, we become less certain that we are not mistaken on the sequence of occurrences, relative importance of various aspects, or the general meaning of the event. For it is well-nigh impossible for two persons who have seen the same event to describe it in exactly the same way when recounting it later on.

Let us turn once more to the life of Henri Brulard. Stendhal recounts that he and two friends, as children, shot a pistol at the Tree of Fraternity. The story is a succession of uncomplicated scenes.

But his friend, R. Colomb, continually pointed out factual errors as he annotated the manuscript.[5]

> The soldiers were almost touching us and we took refuge in the doorway of my grandfather's house, but we could be seen very easily; everybody was at the windows. Many had brought candles and the light shone out.

(But Colomb writes: "Error. All this occurred four minutes after the shot. By that time, all three of us were in the house.")

Stendhal then continues his narrative, recounting how he and one other, perhaps Colomb, had climbed the stairs and taken refuge in the home of two "deeply devout old milliners." The police came. These Jansenist old maids lied, saying that the boys had spent the whole evening there. (Colomb notes: "Only H.B. [Stendhal] entered the home of the Misses Caudey. R.C. [Colomb] and Mante fled through a passage in the attic and managed to reach Main Street.")

> We listened carefully, and when we could no longer hear the police, we departed and continued upstairs toward the passage.

(Colomb writes. "Error!")

> Mante and Treillard, who were more agile than me, . . . told us the next day that when they reached the door on Main Street, they found it blocked by two guards. The boys began to comment on the charm of the young ladies with whom they had spent the evening. The guards asked them no questions and they made their escape.
>
> Their story seems so real to me that at this point I could not be certain that it was not Colomb and I who went out talking about the charm of the young ladies.

(In reality, as Colomb writes, "Treillard was not with us three." And "R.C., having a chest cold, put liquorice in his mouth so that his coughing would not attract the attention of those searching the house. . . . R.C. recalls that there existed in this attic a passageway which was connected to a service staircase leading to Main Street. Remembering this fact saved the two friends. When they got to the street, they saw two men whom they assumed were police officers

---

[5] *Vie d'Henri Brulard*, pp. 365–369.

and they began to calmly and innocently talk about the fun times they had just had.")

> As I write this, the image of the Tree of Fraternity appears before my eyes. My memory is making discoveries. I think that I can see the Tree of Fraternity surrounded by a wall two feet high, faced with hewn stone, and supporting an iron grill five or six feet high.

(Colomb writes, "No.")

It is worthwhile to note in such an example how portions of a narrative which seemed so much clearer than others suddenly change character and become so obscure and uncertain as to allow contradictions when confronted by the remembrances of another witness. Stendhal had filled the gaps in his memory with his imagination. In his story everything seemed believable, and the same light played across the whole surface. But the cracks were revealed when it was viewed from another angle.

Conversely, there is no such thing as an absolute void in memory. No area of our past is so emptied of memory that every image projected there will discover only pure and simple imagination or impersonal historical representation, without ever catching hold of any element of remembrance. We forget nothing, but this proposition may be understood in different ways. According to Bergson, our past in its entirety remains in memory, and only certain obstacles, notably the behavior of the brain, prevents our evoking any and every segment. In any case, the images of past events rest fully formed in the unconscious mind like so many printed pages of books that could be opened, even though they no longer are. In my view, by contrast, what remains are not ready-made images in some subterranean gallery of our thought. Rather, we can find in society all the necessary information for reconstructing certain parts of our past represented in an incomplete and indefinite manner, or even considered completely gone from memory.

When we accidentally meet persons who have participated in these same events, co-actors or witnesses, or when we are told or otherwise discover something about such past happenings, how does it happen that we use these materials to fill in apparent gaps in memory? What we take for an empty space is, in reality, only a somewhat vague area that our thought avoids because so few traces remain. As soon as a precise path to our past is indicated, we see these traces emerge, we link them together, and we see them grow in depth and unity. These traces did exist, therefore, but they were more marked in others' memory than in our own. Certainly we do the reconstructing, but we do so following guidelines laid down by our other remembrances and the remembrances of other people. These new images are triggered by what would remain, without them, other remembrances, undefined and inexplicable though nonetheless real. Similarly, when we travel through older districts of a large city, we experience particular satisfaction in recounting the history of its streets and houses. The area provides many new ideas that, nonetheless, seem quite familiar because they agree with our impressions and fit easily into the present scene. Indeed, the scene seems by itself to evoke them, and what we imagine seems to be an elaboration of what we have just seen. The picture unfolding before us was charged with meaning, which remained obscure although we divined something of it. The character of persons among whom we have lived must be discovered and explained in the light of all the experience we gain in subsequent periods of our life. As this new picture is projected over the facts as we already know them, we see features revealed that then take their place among these facts and receive a clearer meaning. In this way memory is enriched by hitherto alien additions that, once they have taken root and regained their place, are no longer distinguished from other remembrances.

Distant Frameworks and Nearby Milieus

As I have already stated, the remembrances of these groups must have some connection with the events constituting my past if my memory is to be strengthened and completed by the memory of others. Indeed, each of us is at once a member of several groups of varying size. Suppose we turn our attention to the larger groups—

for example, the nation. Although our life, and our parents' and friends' lives, are encompassed within national life, the nation as such can't be said to be interested in the destiny of each of its members. Let us assume that national history is a faithful résumé of the most important events that have changed the life of a nation. It differs from local, state, or city histories in retaining only facts of interest to the citizens as a whole or, if you prefer, citizens as members of the nation. For history of this type, however detailed it may be, to help us conserve and retrieve remembrances of a definite person, he would have to be a historical personage. There are surely times when all men in a country forget their own interests, families, and smaller groups to which their outlook is ordinarily limited. There are events of national import that simultaneously alter the lives of all citizens. Rare as such events might be, they could still offer everyone a few temporal landmarks. Ordinarily, however, the nation is too remote from the individual for him to consider the history of his country as anything else than a very large framework with which his own history makes contact at only a few points. In many novels tracing the destiny of an individual or a family, knowledge of the period during which the action occurs is quite unimportant, and their psychological content would not be lost if the story were set in another period. Inner life would seem to be intensified as it is isolated from those historical circumstances that are paramount in the historical memory. If an author has situated his novel or play in a remote time, hasn't this been an artifice usually intended to set aside the frameworks of contemporary events in order to give us a better feeling for how much the interplay of emotions is independent of historical events? If the historical memory is understood as the sequence of events remembered in national history, then neither it nor its frameworks represent the essence of what I call collective memory.

But between individual and nation lie many other, more restricted groups. Each of these has its own memory. Changes in such a group more directly affect the life and thought of members. The lawyer remembers cases he has presented. The doctor remembers sick people he has cared for. Each recalls fellow professionals with whom he has had contact. As each thinks about all these people, doesn't he go back far into his own personal life? He evokes many thoughts and concerns tied up with the person he once was, the fortunes of his family, and various friendships, with whatever constitutes his personal history. Of course, all this is but one aspect of his life. However, as I have repeatedly noted, each man is immersed successively or simultaneously in several groups. Moreover, each group is confined in space and time. Each has its own original collective memory, keeping alive for a time important remembrances; the smaller the group, the greater the interest members have in these events. Whereas one may easily be lost in the city, village inhabitants continually observe one another. The group memory faithfully registers everything that it can about each member, because these facts react on this small society and help change it. In such milieus all persons think and remember in common. Each has his own perspective, but each is connected so closely to everyone else that, if his remembrances become distorted, he need only place himself in the viewpoint of others to rectify them.

The Ultimate Opposition Between Collective Memory and History

The collective memory is not the same as formal history, and "historical memory" is a rather unfortunate expression because it connects two terms opposed in more than one aspect. Our preceding analysis suggests these conclusions. Undoubtedly, history is a collection of the most notable facts in the memory of man. But past events read about in books and taught and learned in schools are selected, combined, and evaluated in accord with necessities and rules not imposed on the groups that had through time guarded them as a living trust. General history starts only when tradition ends and the social memory is fading or breaking up. So long as a remembrance continues to exist, it is useless to set it down in writing or otherwise fix it in memory. Likewise the need to write the history of a period, a society, or even a person is only aroused when the subject is already too distant in the past to allow for the testimony of those who preserve some remembrance of it. The memory of a sequence of events may no longer have the support of a group: the memory of involvement in the events or of enduring their consequences, of participating in them or receiving a firsthand account from participants and witnesses, may become scattered among various individuals, lost amid new groups for whom these facts no longer have interest because the events are definitely external to them. When this occurs, the only means of preserving such remembrances is to write them down in a coherent narrative, for the writings remain even though the thought and the spoken word die. If a memory exists only when the remembering subject, individual or group, feels that it goes back to its remembrances in a continuous movement, how could history ever be a memory, since there is a break in continuity between the society reading this history and the group in the past who acted in or witnessed the events?

Of course, one purpose of history might just be to bridge the gap between past and present, restoring this ruptured continuity. But how can currents of collective thought whose impetus lies in the past be re-created, when we can grasp only the present? Through detailed study historians can recover and bring to light facts of varying importance believed to be definitely lost, especially if they have the good fortune to discover unpublished memoirs. Nevertheless, when the *Mémoires de Saint-Simon*, for example, were published at the beginning of the nineteenth century, could it be said that French society of 1830 regained contact, a living and direct contact, with the end of the seventeenth century and the time of the Regency? What passed from these memoirs into the basic histories, which have a readership sufficiently widespread to really influence collective opinions? The only effect of such publications is to make us understand how distant we are from those who are doing the writing and being described. The barriers separating us from such a period are not overcome by scattered individuals merely devoting much time and effort to such reading. The study of history in this sense is reserved only for a few specialists. Even were there a group devoted to reading the *Mémoires de Saint-Simon*, it would be much too small to affect public opinion.

History wanting to keep very close to factual details must become erudite, and erudition is the affair of only a very small minority. By contrast, if history is restricted to preserving the image of the past still having a place in the contemporary collective memory, then it retains only what remains of interest to present-day society—that is, very little.

Collective memory differs from history in at least two respects. It is a current of continuous thought whose continuity is not at all artificial, for it retains from the past only what still lives or is capable of living in the consciousness of the groups keeping the memory alive. By definition it does not exceed the boundaries of this group. When a given period ceases to interest the subsequent period, the same group has not forgotten a part of its past, because, in reality, there are two successive groups, one following the other. History divides the sequence of centuries into periods, just as the content of a tragedy is divided into several acts. But in a play the same plot is carried from one act to another and the same characters remain true to form to the end, their feelings and emotions developing in an unbroken movement. History, however, gives the impression that everything—the interplay of interests, general orientations, modes of studying men and events, traditions, and perspectives on the future—is transformed from one period to another. The apparent persistence of the same groups merely reflects the persistence of external distinctions resulting from places, names, and the general character of societies. But the men composing the same group in two successive periods are like two tree stumps that touch at their extremities but do not form one plant because they are not otherwise connected.

Of course, reason sufficient to partition the succession of generations at any given moment is not immediately evident, because the number of births hardly varies from year to year. Society is like a thread that is made from a series of animal or vegetable fibers intertwined at regular intervals; or, rather, it resembles the cloth made from weaving these threads together. The sections of a cotton or silk fabric correspond to the end of a motif or design. Is it the same for the sequence of generations?

Situated external to and above groups, history readily introduces into the stream of facts simple demarcations fixed once and for all. In doing so, history not merely obeys a didactic need for schematization. Each period is apparently considered a whole, independent for the most part of those preceding and following, and having some task—good, bad, or indifferent—to accomplish. Young and old, regardless of age, are encompassed within the same perspective so long as this task has not yet been completed, so long as certain national, political, or religious situations have not yet realized their full implications. As soon as this task is finished and a new one proposed or imposed, ensuing generations start down a new slope, so to speak. Some people were left behind on the opposite side of the mountain, having never made it up. But the young, who hurry as if fearful of missing the boat, sweep along a portion of the older adults. By contrast, those who are located at the beginning of either slope down, even if they are very near the crest, do not see each other any better and they remain as ignorant of one another as they would be were they further down on their respective slope. The farther they are located down their respective slope, the farther they are placed into the past or what is no longer the past; or, alternatively, the more distant they are from one another on the sinuous line of time.

Some parts of this portrait are accurate. Viewed as a whole from afar and, especially, viewed from without by the spectator who never belonged to the groups he observes, the facts may allow such an arrangement into successive and distinct configurations, each period having a beginning, middle, and end. But just as history is interested in differences and contrasts, and highlights the diverse features of a group by concentrating them in an individual, it similarly attributes to an interval of a few years changes that in reality took much longer. Another period of society might conceivably begin on the day after an event had disrupted, partially destroyed, and transformed its structure. But only later, when the new society had already engendered new resources and pushed on to other goals, would this fact be noticed. The historian cannot take these demarcations seriously. He cannot imagine them to have been noted by those who lived during the years so demarcated, in the manner of the character in the farce who exclaims, "Today the Hundred Years War begins!" A war or revolution may create a great chasm between two generations, as if an intermediate generation had just disappeared. In such a case, who can be sure that, on the day after, the youth of society will not be primarily concerned, as the old will be, with erasing any traces of that rupture, reconciling separated generations and maintaining, in spite of everything, continuity of social evolution? Society must live. Even when institutions are radically transformed, and especially then, the best means of making them take root is to buttress them with everything transferable from tradition. Then, on the day after the crisis, everyone affirms that they must begin again at the point of interruption, that they must pick up the pieces and carry on. Sometimes nothing is considered changed, for the thread of continuity has been retied. Although soon rejected, such an illusion allows transition to the new phase without any feeling that the collective memory has been interrupted.

In reality, the continuous development of the collective memory is marked not, as is history, by clearly etched demarcations but only by irregular and uncertain boundaries. The present (understood as extending over a certain duration that is of interest to contemporary society) is not contrasted to the past in the way two neighboring historical periods are distinguished. Rather, the past no longer exists, whereas, for the historian, the two periods have equivalent reality. The memory of a society extends as far as the memory of the groups composing it. Neither ill will nor indifference causes it to forget so many past events and personages. Instead, the groups keeping these remembrances fade away. Were the duration of human life doubled or tripled, the scope of the collective memory as measured in units of time would be more extensive. Nevertheless, such an enlarged memory might well lack richer content if so much tradition were to hinder its evolution. Similarly, were human life shorter, a collective memory covering a lesser duration might never grow impoverished because change might accelerate a society "unburdened" in this way. In any case, since social memory erodes at the edges as individual members, especially older ones, become isolated or die, it is constantly transformed along with the group itself. Stating when a collective remembrance has disappeared and whether it has definitely left group consciousness is difficult, especially since its recovery only requires its preservation in some limited portion of the social body.

History, Record of Events; Collective Memory, Depository of Tradition

In effect, there are several collective memories. This is the second characteristic distinguishing the collective memory from history. History is unitary, and it can be said that there is only one history. Let me explain what I mean. Of course, we can distinguish the history of France, Germany, Italy, the history of a certain period, region, or city, and even that of an individual. Sometimes historical work is even reproached for its excessive specialization and fanatic desire for detailed study that neglects the whole and in some manner takes the part for the whole. But let us consider this matter more closely. The historian justifies these detailed studies by believing that detail added to detail will form a whole that can in turn be added to other wholes; in the total record resulting from all these successive summations, no fact will be subordinated to any other fact, since every fact is as interesting as any other and merits as much to be brought forth and recorded. Now the historian can make such judgments because he is not located within the viewpoint of any genuine and living groups of past or present. In contrast to the historian, these groups are far from affording equal significance to events, places, and periods that have not affected them equally. But the historian certainly means to be objective and impartial. Even when writing the history of his own country, he tries to synthesize a set of facts comparable with some other set, such as the history of another country, so as to avoid any break in continuity. Thus, in the total record of European history, the comparison of the various national viewpoints on the facts is never found; what is found, rather, is the sequence and totality of the facts such as they are, not for a certain country or a certain group but independent of any group judgment. The very divisions that separate countries are historical facts of the same value as any others in such a record. All, then, is on the same level. The historical world is like an ocean fed by the many partial histories. Not surprisingly, many historians in every period since the beginning of historical writing have considered writing universal histories. Such is the natural orientation of the historical mind. Such is the fatal course along which every historian would be swept were he not restricted to the framework of more limited works by either modesty or short-windedness.

Of course, the muse of history is Clio. History can be represented as the universal memory of the human species. But there is no universal memory. Every collective memory requires the support of a group delimited in space and time. The totality of past events can be put together in a single record only by separating them from the memory of the groups who preserved them and by severing the bonds that held them close to the psychological life of the social milieus where they occurred, while retaining only the group's chronological and spatial outline of them. This procedure no longer entails restoring them to lifelike reality, but requires relocating them within the frameworks with which history organizes events. These frameworks are external to these groups and define them by mutual contrast. That is, history is interested primarily in differences and disregards the resemblances without which there would have been no memory, since the only facts remembered are those having the common trait of belonging to the same consciousness. Despite the variety of times and places, history reduces events to seemingly comparable terms, allowing their interrelation as variations on one or several themes. Only in this way does it manage to give us a summary vision of the past, gathering into a moment and symbolizing in a few abrupt changes or in certain stages undergone by a people or individual, a slow collective evolution. In this way it presents us a unique and total image of the past.

In order to give ourselves, by way of contrast, an idea of the multiplicity of collective memories, imagine what the history of our own life would be like were we, in recounting it, to halt each time we recalled some group to which we had belonged, in order to examine its nature and say everything we know about it. It would not be enough to single out just a few groups—for example, our parents, primary school, *lycée*, friends, professional colleagues, social acquaintances, and any political, religious, or artistic circles with which we have been connected. These major spheres are convenient, but they correspond to a still external and simplified view of reality. These groups are composed of much smaller groups, and we have contact with only a local unit of the latter. They change and segment continually. Even though we stay, the group itself actually becomes, by the slow or rapid replacement of its members, another group having only a few traditions in common with its original ones. Having lived a long time in the same city, we have old and new friends; even within our family, the funerals, marriages, and births are like so many successive endings and new beginnings. Of course, these more recent groups are sometimes only branches of a larger group growing in extent and complexity, to which new segments have been joined. Nevertheless, we discern distinct zones within them, and the same currents of thought and sequences of remembrances do not pass through our mind when we pass from one zone to another. That is, the great majority of these groups, even though not currently divided, nevertheless represent, as Leibnitz said, a kind of social material indefinitely divisible in the most diverse directions.

Let us now consider the content of these collective memories. In contrast to history or, if it is preferred, to the historical memory, I do not claim that the collective memory retains only resemblances. To be able to speak of memory, the parts of the period over which it extends must be differentiated in some way. Each of these groups has a history. Persons and events are distinguished. What strikes us about this memory, however, is that resemblances are paramount. When it considers its own past, the group feels strongly that it has remained the same and becomes conscious of its identity through time. History, I have said, is not interested in these intervals when nothing apparently happens, when life is content with repetition in a somewhat different, but essentially unaltered, form without rupture or upheaval. But the group, living first and foremost for its own sake, aims to perpetuate the feelings and images forming the substance of its thought. The greatest part of its memory spans time during which nothing has radically changed. Thus events happening within a family or to its members would be stressed in a written history of the family, though they would have meaning for the kin group only by providing clear proof of its own almost unaltered character, distinctive from all other families. Were a conflicting event, the initiative of one or several members, or, finally, external circumstances to introduce into the life of the group a new element incompatible with its past, then another group, with its own memory, would arise, and only an incomplete and vague remembrance of what had preceded this crisis would remain.

History is a record of changes; it is naturally persuaded that societies change constantly, because it focuses on the whole, and hardly a year passes when some part of the whole is not transformed. Since history teaches that everything is interrelated, each of these transformations must react on the other parts of the social body and prepare, in turn, further change. Apparently the sequence of historical events is discontinuous, each fact separated from what precedes or follows by an interval in which it is believed that nothing has happened. In reality, those who write history and pay primary attention to changes and differences understand that passing from one such difference to another requires the unfolding of a sequence of transformations of which history perceives only the sum (in the sense of the integral calculus) or final result. This viewpoint of history is due to its examining groups from outside and to its encompassing a rather long duration. In contrast, the collective memory is the group seen from within during a period not exceeding, and most often much shorter than, the average duration of a human life. It provides the group a self-portrait that unfolds through time, since it is an image of the past, and allows the group to recognize itself throughout the total succession of images. The collective memory is a record of resemblances and, naturally, is convinced that the group remains the same because it focuses attention on the group, whereas what has changed are the group's relations or contacts with other groups. If the group always remains the same, any changes must be imaginary, and the changes that do occur in the group are transformed into similarities. Their function is to develop the several aspects of one single content—that is, the various fundamental characteristics of the group itself.

Moreover, how would a memory be possible otherwise? It would be paradoxical to claim that the memory preserves the past in the present or introduces the present into the past if they were not actually two zones of the same domain and if the group, insofar as it returns into itself and becomes self-conscious through remembering and isolation from others, does not tend to enclose itself in a relatively immobile form. The group is undoubtedly under the influence of an illusion when it believes the similarities more important than the differences, but it clearly cannot account for the differences, because the images it has previously made of itself are only slowly transformed. But the framework may be enlarged or compressed without being destroyed, and the assumption may be made that the group has only gradually focused on previously unemphasized aspects of itself. What is essential is that the features distinguishing it from other groups survive and be imprinted on all its content. We might have to leave one of these groups for a long time, or the group may break up, its older membership may die off, or a change in our residence, career, or sympathies and beliefs may oblige us to bid it farewell. When we then recall all the times we have spent in the group, do these remembrances not actually come to us as a single piece? So much so that we sometimes imagine the oldest remembrances to be the most immediate; or, rather, they are all illuminated in a uniform light, like objects blending together in the twilight.

3. Time and the Collective Memory

The Social Division of Time

Time often weighs very heavily upon us. We may find a short period of time much too long when, for example, we are impatient, bored, hastening to finish an unpleasant task, or undergoing some physical or moral test. Conversely, we may experience a relatively long duration as much too short—as, for example, when we feel pressed during work or play or when our life progresses from childhood to old age. Sometimes we would like time to flow faster; at other times, we would like it to slow down or come to a standstill. In the first place, we probably resign ourselves to these facts because the speed and rhythm of temporal succession is but the necessary order linking together biological and physical phenomena. Perhaps we come to terms primarily, however, because temporal divisions, with their fixed partitions of duration, derive from conventions and customs and express the order, similarly inevitable, of the successive phases of social life. As Durkheim keenly observed, an isolated individual might, strictly speaking, be unaware of the flow of time and incapable of measuring duration, whereas social life implies that all men agree on times and duration and know well the conventions governing them. This is why there is a collective representation of time. It agrees with the basic facts of astronomy and terrestrial physics. But society superimposes upon these general frameworks others especially suited to the conditions and habits of concrete human groups. Indeed, in a manner of speaking, astronomical dates and divisions of time have been so overlaid by social demarcations as to gradually disappear, nature having increasingly left to society the job of organizing duration.

Moreover, men adjust quite easily to whatever temporal demarcations are used because these are generally traditional, and each year or day occurs with the same temporal structure as those preceding it, like so many fruit from the same tree. It's futile to complain that such demarcations upset one's habits, for the constraint experienced is of a quite different character. First of all, the uniformity weighs upon us. Time is similarly divided for all members of society. Perhaps we find it disagreeable that every Sunday the city has an air of idleness, streets are empty or full of strange people, and we are distracted from doing anything when we would just as soon work. Is it as a protest against this common law that many people, many social milieus, many urban districts, turn night into day? Or that those who can afford it seek out the warmth of southern France in midwinter? Our need to differ from others in the way we divide and regulate time would probably grow were we not socially disciplined in our occupation and recreation. I must go to my office during business hours, when the other employees are present. The division of labor involves men in a mechanical interlinking of activities. The more it progresses, the more it requires we be on time. I have to be on time to attend a concert or play, to make a train, or to ensure that other guests are not kept waiting at a dinner. I must regulate my activities by a clock or in accord with a rhythm adopted by others without consideration of my own preferences. I must be frugal with my time and never waste it, because I might jeopardize certain opportunities or advantages that life in society offers. But what is probably more painful is that I feel perpetually constrained to consider life, and the events filling it, in terms of measurement. I anxiously reflect on my age, expressed as the number of years lived and remaining. It is as if life were a blank page divided into equal parts by so many lines or, better, as if the years ahead of me shrank in proportion as the elapsed time of my life increased. Indeed, we become so used to measuring time in order to use it fully that we no longer know what to do with those portions of duration not so measured, when we are on our own and outside the current of external social life, as it were. These could become so many cases where we momentarily forget time but rediscover ourselves. Quite to the contrary, we are aware of what are really empty intervals, and our problem is knowing how to pass time. In obliging us to continually measure life in its way, society actually renders us increasingly incapable of organizing it in our own way. Time wasted doubtless remains for some people what is regretted least (or, in another sense, what is regretted most). But such people are the exception.

Bergson's Doctrine of Pure (Individual) Duration and "Common Time"

Assuming its existence, what is the source of this social time that imposes its divisions on individual consciousness? One view holds it reasonable to distinguish time or duration itself from its divisions. More precisely, every human being endowed with consciousness has a feeling of duration because various mental states flow in succession within him. Duration is nothing else than the sequence of these states, the current that seems to pass through and beneath them, giving rise to one after another. In this sense each man has his own appropriate duration, an original datum of consciousness that is known directly without the need for any externally introduced conception. Since these states are distinct, it is even possible to perceive natural divisions in this sequence, corresponding to the passage from one state to another, from one continuous series of similar states to another like sequence. Moreover, since we perceive external objects—and nature shows many regularities, such as the succession of days and nights or the succession of footsteps tracing our movement—an isolated individual can attain the concept of measureable time solely by his own powers and based solely on the data of his own experience.

But certain objects are a meeting place for the thoughts of individuals. In any case, we picture those we meet in voice and gesture as having a sensory existence in space. Thus sections are cut out in both my duration and theirs that tend to extend to the durations or consciousnesses of other individuals (even to all people). We can imagine some kind of empty time to unfold between these successive common moments that we are assumed to remember—a common casing for the lived duration of the personal consciousness, as the psychologist might say. We find it convenient to measure time by periodic natural movements of heavenly bodies or by creating artificial regulators such as watches because we are unable to find in the sequence of conscious states enough definite points of reference valid for every consciousness.

In effect, the essence of individual duration is to have a content different from any other, so that its stream of mental states varies in rapidity, within itself over time as well as in relation to any other. There are the slack hours and empty days. There is also the acceleration of events, quickened reflection, heightened emotion, which make us feel we have lived years in just a few hours or days. The same contrast holds between individuals. For every lively mind, tense and impatient, how many more do we find slow and monotonous, rarely stimulated by events, the result of a lagging interest in fewer things? Perhaps a growing disinterest, a progressive weakening of emotion, explains why the rhythm of inner life dims with age. A child's day is filled with multiplying impressions and observations, comprising many moments as it were. The old person's day, by contrast—if account be taken only of its real content, of what has awakened attention and made us feel our inner life—amounts to far fewer states distinct from one another, to a few rather dilated moments. The old person who still remembers childhood now finds his days at once slower and shorter. Time seems to flow more slowly because moments as he lives them feel longer; then again, it seems to flow more rapidly because moments as normally reckoned, or as measured by watch, follow in such rapid succession as to pass him by. The space of his day cannot accommodate everything that a child easily fits in, because his inner duration has slowed. Hence a child and an older person who shared no other means to measure time than their feeling of duration and its divisions could never agree on temporal demarcations. The length of the interval chosen as a common unit would seem too small for the child, too large for the adult. We are better off to fix temporal divisions by changes and movements of physical bodies sufficiently periodic to use as a reference. But the idea for this choice is not ours alone. We must come to an understanding with others in this matter.

In reality, all material phenomena provide ourselves and others (because we see them at the same time) the opportunity to verify not only that there is a relationship of simultaneity between certain of our perceptions—that is, our thoughts—but also, and more important, that this relationship occurs at regular intervals that we agree to consider as equal. From then on, conventional temporal divisions are imposed upon us from outside, though they originated in the thought of individuals. Such individuals have merely realized that they meet and adopt an identical attitude toward the same external object, an attitude that recurs periodically. The convention resulting from this process enables us to fix discontinuous reference points, partially external to every consciousness because common to all. But these thoughts have not created a new, impersonal duration that fills up the interval between the moments chosen as reference points. That is, they have not created a collective or social time that would include and interrelate all the components of each duration into one whole. In reality, there is in this interval cut out by these reference points only separate thoughts, with many currents of distinct thought each having its particular duration. We may imagine, if we wish, an empty time within which each duration would flow and be divided up by identical cuts. Indeed, such a conception forces itself on all thought, but it is no more than an abstract representation, which would no longer correspond to any reality if the individual durations ceased to exist.

Let us consider matters, therefore, from a Bergsonian point of view. Universal time, conceived as encompassing every human being and every successive series of phenomena, really amounts to no more than a discontinuous sequence of moments. Each moment corresponds to a relationship established between persons whose thoughts simultaneously become aware of one another. Ordinarily isolated from one another, these thoughts go outside themselves whenever their paths intersect; they momentarily merge into a larger representation encompassing every consciousness and its relationships. In this consists simultaneity. The totality of these moments constitutes a framework we may legitimately adapt, standardize, and simplify. The time separating these moments is empty and may be divided in a multitude of ways. Time is like a blank sheet on which an indefinite number of parallel lines may be drawn. Along that abstract, temporal line joining any two moments (which can be represented as a uniform movement or change completed between them), temporal divisions—such as years, months, days, hours, minutes, or seconds—are established in this manner. Nothing prevents our imagining further simultaneities at some other point one fourth, one third, or one half the way in between. After all, we can presume that people have contact at each of these precise moments that demarcate the hours and even the minutes; and temporal divisions merely symbolize all these possibilities. There is no clearer proof that the time conceived to include all human beings is artificial, created from the addition, combination, and multiplication of data derived solely from the duration of individuals.

A Critique of Bergsonian Subjectivism

However, if these temporal divisions are not contained and specified beforehand in consciousness, is the encounter of two (or more) consciousnesses sufficient to cause their emergence? It is necessary to emphasize this proposition or postulate, because it reveals most clearly the peculiar conception of duration underlying the claim that memory is an individual faculty.

We are urged to discard and erase whatever reminds us of space and external objects in order to gain awareness of our inner and personal thought. Its states, flowing one after another, are quite diverse and distinct, but in a totally different manner from material things. Caught up in a continuously flowing current, they are not clearly demarcated from one another. But this is exactly what characterizes memory or, rather, that truly psychic and active memory that is never confused with habit. Memory (in this sense) has a grip on past mental states and provides us their former reality only because it does not confound them either with one another or with earlier or later states. That is, memory bases itself on differences. Clearly separated and distinct states are doubtless different by that fact alone. Nevertheless, as each state is separated and removed from that current—which would certainly be its lot if we considered each as a distinct reality with sharply defined contours in time— how could it remain totally different from every other state similarly set aside and delimited? Any separation of this type would mean projecting these states into space. But objects in space, however different, admit many resemblances. Their positions, though distinct, are part of a homogeneous milieu. Attributed differences arise from participation in common categories. By contrast, the current within which thoughts flow in inner consciousness is not a homogeneous milieu, since form is not distinguished from matter and container and content are one. In these "conscious states" (this term is itself inadequate, for there are actually no states but only movements or thought in ceaseless becoming), qualities can be distinguished only by abstraction because, in essence, each state is unified and is a viewpoint over all consciousness. They have no categories in common because each is unique. Any effort at comparison disrupts the continuity of the series. It is this very continuity that explains how some states can recall others that precede or follow, just as we drag along the whole chain even if we grab just one link. These individual states form a continuous series because they are all different, and any resemblance or repetition introduces an element of discontinuity. Remembrances also evoke one another because they are different. Otherwise the series would be incomplete and broken at each moment.

But if this were the case, it is difficult to understand how two individual consciousnesses could ever come in contact, how two series of equally continuous states would manage to intersect—which would be necessary if I am to be aware of the simultaneity of two changes, one occurring in myself and the other in the consciousness of someone else. Of course, when I perceive external objects, I may assume that their entire reality is exhausted in the perception I form of them. What is in duration is not objects but my thoughts that represent the objects to me, as I never go outside myself. But it is quite another matter when a human form, a voice or gesture, reveals the presence of a thought other than my own. I then have in mind the representation of an object from two points of view, my own and that of another who, like myself, has a consciousness and endures in time. But how could this be if I am sealed up in my consciousness, if I cannot go outside my duration? If, as this doctrine maintains, my conscious states flow in uninterrupted succession, if they are bound so closely that there are no lines of demarcation among them, if there are no obstacles in the current, if no object with definite contours stands out on the surface of my conscious life—then indeed I cannot go outside my duration.

It might be replied that what breaks the continuity of my individual consciousness is the external action of another consciousness, which imposes upon me a representation containing something of itself. A person crosses my path and forces me to note his presence. Nonetheless, material objects are also imposed on my perceptions from outside. If it is assumed that I am enclosed in myself and know nothing of the external world, however, this sensory perception would no more halt the flow of my mental states than some affective impression or random thought would—it would be incorporated without my having to go outside myself. In this theory of consciousness reduced to contemplating its own states, the same holds true were I to become aware of a human form, to perceive a voice or gesture. The train of individual thought would be undisturbed, and I would never have the idea of another duration besides my own. For it to be otherwise, the object would have to act as a sign for me. But this would imply that I am always capable, in the presence of an object, of putting myself simultaneously in my own viewpoint and in that of another. It implies that, as I imagine the possibility of these other consciousnesses and of their entering into relationship, I also represent a duration common to them all.

We have presupposed a self-enclosed consciousness, whose perceptions are so many subjective states that reveal nothing about the existence of objects. How would its thought ever attain knowledge of the external world? Under these conditions, such knowledge can be gained from neither within nor without. All sensory perception must then be credited with a tendency to self-exteriorization. Thought is made to emerge from the restricted circle of individual consciousness within which it flows and to envisage the object as simultaneously represented in at least one other consciousness (or as capable of being so represented at any moment). But this, in turn, presupposes a prior representation of a "society of consciousnesses." What about these conscious states that, unlike sensory perceptions, do not relate to an external reality? Affective states in their pure form, for example. Do they gain their purely "inward" character from the fact that this representation common to several consciousnesses is absent? Is it not, rather, that this representation is provisionally masked? Isn't it true that actions exerted on us from outside deny it an opportunity to emerge, although it is always latent behind our apparently most personal impressions? For example, we are preoccupied with a physical pain which has lasted for some time, so that our present suffering seems but to prolong and borrow the substance of the past pain. Now suppose we discover that our pain is caused by a physical action (external or organic), that we are only imagining it, or that we even think others are experiencing or could experience the same pain. Then our impression would be at least partially transformed into what might be called an objective representation of the pain. But how could the representation emerge from the impression if it were not already contained in it? Since that representation's very character derives from being common to more than one consciousness, since it is collective only to the extent that it is objective, must we not think that our previous concept of the pain (which is all that is retained in the remembrance of it), if not the pain itself, could be only an incomplete and truncated collective representation?

In this way we might doubtless interpret anew Leibniz's old metaphysical paradox about physical pain, and sensations in general, being confused or incomplete ideas. The pain may not gradually diminish only because we can clearly represent its character and causation. Rather, by imagining that the pain can be experienced and understood by others (impossible were it a personal and hence unique impression), we seem to transfer some of its burden to others, who help us to bear it. The tragic character of pain—the fact that, beyond a certain point, it creates in us a desperate feeling of anxiety and powerlessness—results from our being unable to come to grips with an evil whose cause is within those regions of ourselves inaccessible to others. We are one with our pain, and pain cannot destroy itself. Hence we instinctively search out an intelligible explanation of our suffering; that is, we find an explanation agreeable to the members of our group. Similarly, the witch doctor relieves the patient by pretending to remove from his body a stone, old bone, liquid, or some pointed object. Or we may strip suffering of its mystery by uncovering those aspects of it directed at the consciousness of others. When we represent pain as having been or able to be experienced by our fellow man, we relegate it to a common domain and restore its collective and familiar character.

Thus a deeper analysis of the idea of simultaneity leads us to discard the hypothesis of purely individual and mutually inaccessible durations. The sequence of our mental states is not a line without thickness in which each element connects only to the one preceding and following it. In reality, many currents that proceed back and forth between one consciousness and another crisscross at each moment or stage of the unfolding of our thought. Consciousness is the point of intersection. The apparent continuity of what is called our inner life is due partly to going along such a current, a course of thought unfolding, in others as well as ourself, a particular inclination of collective thought. It also derives from the interrelationship continually established among those of our mental states that derive primarily from the continuity of our organic functioning. Moreover, these two differ in degree only, for affective impressions tend to blossom into collective images and representations. In any case, individual durations are able to establish a larger and impersonal duration encompassing them all because they have themselves separated from their foundation in a collective time that provided their very substance.

The Date: Framework of Remembrance

I have spoken of collective time in contradistinction to individual duration. Without prejudging the question, we must now ask whether collective time is unique. The theory under challenge posits, on the one hand, as many durations as individuals and, on the other, an abstract time encompassing them all. This time is empty and may be only an idea. The partitions that we mark there as intersections of several durations are not the same as states observed to be simultaneous. These demarcations cannot differ from the time they divide—a time conceived as a homogeneous medium, a form bereft of matter. But, then, what kind of reality can be attributed to this form? And, more important, how is it able to serve as a framework for events situated within it?

A time defined in this way can be subdivided in any way whatsoever. Is this why we can assign every event a place within it? Before responding to this question, we must note that here time has significance only insofar as it permits us to retain and recall events occurring within it. This is the service we expect it to perform. For past events this certainly is the case. In recalling a certain trip we have taken, we find ourselves with a whole framework of temporal facts somehow related to it, even when we cannot remember its exact date. For instance, it took place before or after the war, when a child, youth, or adult, in the company of a certain friend who was himself a certain age, during a specific season of the year, while engaged in a certain piece of work, or when some famous event was in the news. A series of reflections of this kind very often enable one to substantiate and complete such a remembrance. If uncertainty about its date still remains, the fact that it belongs to a different period from the other remembrances localizes it after a fashion. However, since a trip might well have been an isolated event unrelated to the rest of our life, it is probably not the best example to use. As we shall see, a spatial and not a temporal framework predominates in this kind of example. By contrast, a temporal framework will probably help us best remember an event occurring in a group that is a continual focus of thought, such as a family or an occupational group. It is the same for upcoming events that we prearrange. The appointment time serves as a reminder of a future meeting. What reminds us of an imminent visit with a parent or friend, of a task to be completed or an important step to be taken, of a promised vacation, is the date scheduled for these events. Sometimes we reconstitute the temporal framework only after the remembrance reappears. We are then obliged to carefully examine the remembrance in order to retrieve the date of its occurrence. Even then we may have recalled the remembrance only because it preserved traces of that period to which it refers and we spotted these traces and thought about that time when the event occurred. This localization, approximate and very crude at first, was then made more precise when the remembrance reappeared. Nevertheless, in most cases we retrieve the image of a past event by mentally traversing the framework of time—but that means time must be suitable for enframing our remembrances.

Abstract Time and Real Time

First of all, let us consider time as conceived in its most abstract form, as that totally homogeneous time of mechanics or physics, which is permeated with geometry and can be called "mathematical time." As the polar opposite of his "lived time," Bergson considers it "void of consciousness." A concept of this type gains interest because it represents the limit men tend to approach as they leave behind their own particular thoughts to place themselves within more extensive groups and totalities. Time must be gradually emptied of matter that might differentiate its various parts, so that it can be used by increasing numbers of people who differ from one another. What might guide thought in this effort to enlarge and universalize time is the latent representation of a wholly uniform milieu, very similar if not identical to the representation of space. Human beings we are told, are geometers by nature, because they live in space. Therefore it is not surprising that, in abstracting from particular events experienced by the individual consciousness, we represent time as a homogeneous medium similar to geometric space.

But could our memory have any grip on a time conceptualized in this way? Where could remembrances adhere on so sleek a surface? Citing Leibniz once again, we might say that such a time provides no rationale for placing a given event at a specific place within it, since its parts are indiscernible from one another. Indeed, mathematical time is concerned only with objects or phenomena that are not fixed and retained in real time, with facts lacking a date but possessing a constant character whenever they occur. In representing successive increments of time starting from zero by the symbols t_0, t_1, $t_2 \ldots t_n$, we certainly specify a duration and the phases of a movement; but we determine a movement that obeys the same law whenever it is reproduced. In other words, the initial moment, t_0, is entirely free of connection with a given moment of real time. The laws of physical movement are in this sense independent of time. Hence mathematicians prefer to resituate such movements in an entirely empty duration and thus represent in singular fashion this paradox of a movement that is clearly in time because it has duration, but is, nevertheless, not situated at any definite moment. With the exception of the society of mathematicians and scientists studying the movements of inert bodies, every human group is interested in events whose character and importance depend on the moment of their occurrence. An indefinite time of this type, indifferent to its content, would be of no help to the memory of such groups.

Of course, we may seem to appeal to a representation of this time when we divide time into equal intervals. Nonetheless, days, hours, minutes, and seconds are not mere divisions of a homogeneous time, for they actually have a definite collective meaning. They are so many reference points in a duration whose various parts are differentiated and noninterchangeable in common thought. When we learn that a certain train leaves at 1500 hours, we are obliged to translate this fact and remember that the train in reality departs at three o'clock in the afternoon. Similarly, we distinguish the 30th or 31st of the month from the first day of the next month even more (or, at least, in a different way) than we do the first day from the second, or the fifteenth day from the sixteenth. Even as we focus attention on the numerals themselves, we do not consider them so many arbitrary dividers that can be modified at will, much as mechanics shifts the origin or alters the system of axes. It is something quite different to pass from standard time to daylight savings and agree to call noon one o'clock. The group does not readily give up its normal time: social life does not abandon its temporal framework but accompanies such alterations. Such is the sensitivity of social time to demarcations introduced into it. Hence, no more than individual duration is social time to be confused with mathematical time. There is a fundamental opposition between real time, individual or social, and abstract time. It is incorrect to say that real time approaches mathematical time as it becomes more social.

"Universal Time" and "Historical Times"

What might be called "universal time," encompassing all events that have occurred in the world, on all continents, in all countries, to all groups within each country, and thus to all individuals, may now seem more concrete and definite to us. All men can be pictured as one vast totality. This whole shows only a very imperfect organic unity—less imperfect in the present, however, than in the past. But its parts nonetheless form one continuous whole, because they have probably had at least sporadic contact with one another. Thus, each has gradually become attached to the whole by bonds which vary in strength. Of course, this statement is not strictly accurate. Certain long-inhabited regions have only recently been discovered. There are also peoples we know only from vague traditions and brief narratives of travelers. They do not have a history in the sense of past events with determinate dates, even though they keep memories of such events. We nevertheless acknowledge these events as contemporaneous with those known in our own civilization, and all we lack are the written documents, annals, or monument inscriptions to situate them in the same time as our own history. We encounter once again that historical time of which I spoke in the preceding chapter, except that we now assume that it extends beyond the previously recognized limits to the life of peoples having no history and even to prehistory.

However natural such an extension may be, we must still ascertain its legitimacy. What possible meaning could this time have for us when various peoples, including the oldest of which we have knowledge, have preserved no remembrances? Of course, we can always reason by analogy. We might postulate, for example, that Mars has always been inhabited. Would we assert, however, that the Martians have lived in the same time as the peoples of earth whose history we know? For such a proposition to have a clearly defined meaning, we must further suppose that the Martians have somehow been able to communicate with us, at least intermittently, so that each party has been in contact with the other and has some knowledge of the other's life and history. Otherwise we would have a situation similar to that of two sealed consciousnesses whose durations never intersect. How, in such a case, may we speak of a time common to both?

But we must pursue this matter further. Let us consider only those past events whose date and temporal ordering have been approximately determined by historians. Does the historian's record of simultaneous events occurring in countries and regions distant from one another permit us to conclude that a universal time really exists within the limits of history? We commonly speak about historical "times" as if there were several. Perhaps such terms are intended to designate successive periods closer or farther from the present. But we can give another meaning to this expression. There might be several "histories," which begin at different times and are distinct from one another. Of course, the historian can position himself outside and above these parallel evolutions and consider them all as so many facets of one universal history. But we may feel that in many, perhaps most, cases the unity he achieves is wholly artificial because events that had no influence on one another, and peoples who have never shared a common thought (even temporarily), are brought together and compared.

Before me is Dreyss's *Chronologie Universelle*, published in Paris in 1858. The most notable events occurring in various geographical areas from the remotest past to the present are here laid out year by year. We will skip over the first period, which starts with the creation of the world and ends with the Great Flood. After all, the tradition of a Great Flood is found among many different peoples. It may correspond to a vague memory of a common event and might therefore merit an initial position in a synchronic record of the destiny of nations. In the next period, up to the time of Jesus and even to the fifth century after his death, the author merely outlines the history of the Greeks, Romans, Jews, and Egyptians and juxtaposes these segments. This is only a small part of the whole world. But at least these peoples are proximate enough to be affected by what happens to any one of them. News and ideas did circulate between their cities, remote from each other though they were. By 1858, and even before, the historical horizon had definitely broadened. Many more regions could have been included within this old chronologic framework. Nevertheless, with all its limitations, this survey may very well provide an image better approximating reality. For it shows a set of peoples with closely intertwined destinies, whose changes of fortune fitted within a common time. The world may be only that known to the ancients, but at least it nearly forms a whole.

As Dreyss's chronology approaches modern times, it gradually loses in unity what it gains in breadth. We are told that in 1453 both the Hundred Years War ends and the Turks conquer Constantinople. What common collective memory retains traces of both those events? Everything is interrelated, of course, and we cannot at the time predict the spatial extent of the repercussions of a given event. But the memory of a people records only the repercussions affecting them and not the events themselves. It matters little that certain events occurred the same year if that simultaneity was not noted by contemporaries. Each locally defined group has its own memory and its own representation of time. Cities, provinces, or peoples unite, and the common time grows and extends further into the past, at least for those elements of the new group who now participate in traditions more ancient than their own. The reverse may also occur, when a nation disintegrates, a colony is formed, or a new continent is populated. America's history from the first settlements to the beginning of the nineteenth century was intimately bound to Europe's, whereas the two appear separate from the nineteenth century to the present. How can a people with only a short history behind them represent time as do others with a memory going far into the past? These two times have been related only by an artificial construction. They have been laid alongside one another on an empty time without historical reality—in brief, on a time that is nothing more than the abstract time of the mathematician.

Of course, we ought not forget that even in an epoch of sparse communication, when neither telegraph nor newspapers existed, people nonetheless traveled about and news circulated farther and more rapidly than we might suppose. The Church spanned all Europe and even had antennas on other continents. A well-developed diplomatic system enabled princes and ministers to know rather quickly what occurred in other countries. Merchants had warehouses, branches, shops, and agents in foreign cities. Certain groups and milieus served as liaisons between the most distant countries. But the horizon of the masses was scarcely broadened. For a long time most men were seldom interested in what happened outside the borders of their province, let alone their country. That is why there existed, and still do, as many histories as nations. Within the viewpoint of what body of people will that person stand who aspires to write universal history and yet avoid these restrictions? Is this why the main events emphasized in historical narratives were for a long time matters of interest to the Church, such as councils, schisms, papal successions, and the conflict between clerical and temporal leaders, or to diplomats, such as negotiations, alliances, wars, treaties, and court intrigues? Is this not why in more recent times, when the social circles of merchants, businessmen, industrialists, and bankers have extended their sway over the greater portion of the earth, universal history has made room for the progress of industry, commercial changes, and international economic relations? But a universal history so conceived is still but a juxtaposition of partial histories embracing a limited number of groups. Even if the unique time thus reconstructed extends over vast spaces, it still includes but a narrow part of the humanity peopling this earth. The masses, who also occupy these regions but who never enter into these restricted social circles, also have their own history.

Historical Chronology and
Collective Tradition

Perhaps we have taken up a viewpoint that is not, and can never be, the historian's. We fault him for confounding within a unitary time national and local histories that really constitute distinctive lines of evolution, as it were. A synchronic record, by collating events without regard to their location of occurrence, clearly separates these events from their milieus, which situated them in a time characteristic to the milieu concerned. That is, the events are considered independent of the real time to which they belong. Current opinion, on the contrary, holds that history is perhaps too exclusively concerned with the chronological succession of facts. But let me restate my contrast of "historical memory" and "collective memory" from the previous chapter. The first retains primarily differences. But differences or changes merely mark the sudden, almost immediate, passage from a given state that endures to another that endures. By the abstracting from states or intervals in order to retain only their boundaries or limits, what is omitted is actually the more substantial part of time itself. A change clearly extends over a duration, occasionally a very long one. This is tantamount to saying that the change is broken up into a series of partial changes separated by intervals without change. The historical narrative abstracts even more from these smaller intervals. Moreover, it could not possibly do anything else. If we are to adequately understand what does not change, what endures in the true sense of the term, we must be placed within the social milieu that was aware of that relative stability and made to relive a collective memory now extinct. Does it suffice to describe an institution and tell us it has not changed during half a century? First of all, such a description would be inaccurate. Many slow and imperceptible alterations have occurred, of which the historian is unaware, but which the groups sense along with the relative stability (for these two representations are always intimately bound together). Furthermore, such a description is by consequence a purely negative datum. We are never made to know the content of the group consciousness or the various circumstances within which this group was still able to recognize that the institution had indeed not changed. History is necessarily an abridgment; hence it compresses and concentrates into a few instants developments extending over entire periods. In this sense it extracts changes from duration. There is nothing to prevent our collating together events thus separated from real time and organizing them into a chronological series. But such a series unfolds within an artificial duration having no reality for the groups from which these events are borrowed. This is not the time in which their collective thought habitually functioned or localized what was remembered of their past.

Multiplicity and Heterogeneity of Collective Durations

Depending on the group, the collective memory goes back into the past a varying distance. Beyond this point it no longer grasps events and persons directly. Now what lies beyond this limit is precisely what draws the historian's attention. History, it is said, is interested in the past, not the present. But what is truly the past for history is what is no longer included within the sphere of thought of existing groups. Apparently history must wait until old groups have disappeared, until their thoughts and memory have vanished, before becoming concerned to fix the image and temporal order of facts that only it can now preserve. Of course, the historian requires the aid of those traces of testimony about the past found in memoirs, newspapers, and official documents. But the historian is guided in his selection and evaluation by reasons having little to do with the opinion of that time, which no longer exists. He is not obliged to take it into account, nor need he fear that it will contradict him. The historian can truly achieve his task only by deliberately placing himself outside the time lived by those groups that participated in the events concerned, which have a more or less direct contact with these events and can recall them.

Let us now place ourselves within the viewpoint of a collective consciousness, the only way we can remain within a real time having enough continuity to enable thought to move throughout without losing sense of its own unity. As shown earlier, we must distinguish as many collective times as there are distinct groups. This is not to deny that social life as a whole flows within a time divided into years, months, days, and hours. Were it otherwise, there would be no way to interrelate the movements of various groups that might well subdivide their durations differently. It is precisely because individuals must move between these groups, each separate and having its own characteristic movement, that temporal demarcations must be sufficiently uniform. When we are within one group, we must always be able to anticipate the time of our entrance into another in terms of its time. But when we are in the first group, we are within its time and not the time of the second. Hence the problem posed for the traveler who must go to a foreign country and yet prefers to keep his watch on his own country's time. Yet he will be guaranteed not missing his train if the two countries are on the same time or he has a time conversion table.

Should we then conclude that there is a unique and universal time to which all groups refer? Its temporal divisions would be imposed on every group. This common pulse, transmitted throughout the social world, would restore communication and relationships that group barriers tend to prevent. First of all, however, the correlation between temporal demarcations in neighboring groups is much less exact than that in an international railway timetable. The requirements of various groups in this regard are not identical. Time has greater flexibility in the family than in the barracks or classroom. While the priest must say his mass at the appointed hour, there is no specific duration for his sermon. With the exception of religious ceremonies, the faithful may go to church for prayers and devotion when they wish, without a time schedule, and even for ceremonies they often arrive late or leave early. A merchant must arrive on time for a business meeting, but sales are made throughout the day and orders and deliveries have very flexible time limits. Moreover, the individual seems to balance the temporal exactitude required by some milieus with the laxity found in others. A group whose elements continually change in relation to one another is the people moving about on the streets. Some no doubt are in a hurry, so they quicken their step, or glance at their watches as they stand on the depot steps or in the entrance or exit of an office building. But, generally, when we are on the streets, we meander about, glancing at magazine stands, not counting the hours or caring what time it is. When we have a long walk to arrive somewhere on time, we are guided by a vague sense of the correct direction and need not pay attention to street names. Since a person need not measure time with the same exactitude in each milieu, the correlation between the times of the office, the home, the street, and the visit turns out to be fixed only within rather broad limits. Hence we apologize for arriving late at a meeting or returning home at an unusual hour by saying that we ran into someone in the street. This amounts to claiming freedom with regard to how we measure time in a milieu that is little concerned with temporal exactitude.

So far I have spoken primarily about hours and minutes. But we sometimes say to a friend, "I'll come to see you one of these days, next week or next month." When we see a distant relative again, we reckon the approximate number of years since we last saw him. This type of relationship or group does not require a more definite determination of dates. From this standpoint, therefore, our modern society has not a single time but several times in varying degrees of correspondence to one another.

Every such time, of course, draws its inspiration from and refers back to a common model, to a single framework that might be considered as the social time *par excellence*. We need not seek out the source of the division of duration into years, months, weeks, and days. In the form we know it, however, it is very old and based on tradition. It apparently resulted from an agreement among all groups, which suggests that at some moment they abolished the barriers separating them and consolidated into a single society for the purpose of demarcating duration. But it is possible, indeed necessary, that such an agreement was achieved in one society from which derive all the others we know of. Let us suppose that religious beliefs once shaped institutions profoundly. Perhaps the men who combined the powers of king and priest divided time under the dual influence of their religious conceptions and their observation of patterns in celestial and terrestrial phenomena. When political and religious groupings were differentiated, when the number of families increased, time remained demarcated as it had been in the original community. New groupings—enduring or ephemeral relationships of people in the same occupation, village, or city, or of friends engaged in social tasks, artistic activity, or just "getting together"—are always formed by separation from older and larger groups. Naturally, many characteristics and concepts from the parent community are retained in these new formations. The demarcation of time is one such tradition that must be carried over, because every group has need to distinguish and recognize the various segments of its duration. Hence the names of the days of the week reveal many traces of extinct traditions and beliefs. Years are dated from the birth of Christ, and old religious ideas about the virtue of the number 12 are the source of the present division of the day into hours, minutes, and seconds.

But the existence of these temporal divisions does not prove that there is only one social time, for their common origin has not prevented their acquiring quite different meanings in different groups. It is not only that the need for exactitude in these matters varies by group (as I have shown). More important, time is counted from different dates in the various groups because these temporal demarcations are applied to sequences of events or actions varying in character, length, and beginning and end points. The academic year and the religious year do not begin on the same day. The anniversary of Christ's birth and of his death and resurrection determine the essential divisions of the Christian year. The secular year begins on the first of January but entails quite different divisions depending on occupation and type of activity. The divisions of the farmer's year are governed by the characteristic agricultural task, which is itself a function of the season. The business year is broken into periods of intense activity and high volume of sales and slack periods, which in turn vary by the industrial or commercial activity concerned. The military year may be calculated from either the date of enlistment or from the time remaining until separation—perhaps the very monotony of the days makes this duration most closely resemble a homogeneous time whose measurement is entirely a matter of convention. Thus there are as many sources of time as there are groups. No single time is imposed on all groups. The individual day is similarly structured. Conceivably the alternation of day and night could mark a fundamental division, an elementary rhythm of time, for every society. Night is for sleep and indeed interrupts social life: man almost totally escapes the grip of laws, customs, and collective representations, and he is truly alone. Nonetheless, is the night an exceptional period in this regard? Is physical sleep unique in being able to temporarily arrest the flow of these currents that make up groups? To attribute to night and physical sleep such a property is to forget that society is not one but many groups whose life is interrupted at times other than nightfall. A group could be said to "fall asleep," as it were, whenever its members are not associating for the purpose of sustaining and developing its thought. But it continues to exist even as it "slumbers," so long as members are ready to gather again and recompose it as it was before their dispersal. Now the only group of which it might be said that its conscious life is periodically suspended by man's physical sleep is the family, for we take leave of family members when going to bed and see them first upon awakening. But the group consciousness of the family pales and even vanishes at other moments also. The father and occasionally the mother go to work, and the children go to school. Such absences, while shorter in clock time than the night, may very well seem as long to the family, which has no awareness of time at night (a man, on waking, does not know how long he has slept, whether one hour or ten, a minute or an eternity). As for other groups, life is generally interrupted well before nightfall and resumed well after daybreak. Moreover, while this interruption may be longer, it does not differ in nature from other breaks occurring in group life at other moments of the day. The workday does not extend continuously from dawn to dusk, for it touches neither boundary and is interrupted by periods devoted to other groups. With even more reason does this apply to the religious day or the social calendar. Night nevertheless seems the essential temporal division because it is so for that group to which we are most closely attached, our family. But we are also attached to other groups whose life stops and starts. Now assume the periods of stoppage were as empty as night and the representation of time disappeared as completely. It would be very difficult to state when the day began and ended for such a group, and it certainly would never happen simultaneously in them all.

Nonetheless, there is a rather exact correspondence between all these times, even though it cannot be said that they have been adjusted to one another by mutually agreed-upon convention. All the groups divide time in roughly the same way because they have inherited the same tradition. Moreover, this traditional partition of duration accords with nature because it was set up by men who observed the patterns of movement of the sun and stars. Every group can verify that the rhythm of social time and the regularity of natural phenomena are well adapted to one another, since all groups are influenced by the same astronomical conditions. It is also true, however, that these temporal demarcations, which are in agreement, are not identical, nor do they always have the same meaning. Everything happens as if all portions of the social body were governed by something similar to the balance wheel of a watch. But there is, in reality, no unique and external calendar to which groups refer. There are as many calendars as different groups because the temporal divisions are expressed, for example, in religious terms (each day consecrated to a saint) or in business terminology ("payday"). That days, months, or years are spoken of matters very little. One group cannot use another's calendar. The merchant does not live or find his reference points in the religious group. If this was the case at various times in the past—if fairs and markets were held on religiously consecrated days, for example, or if the expiration of a commercial debt was placed on St. John's feast day or on Candlemas— it was because the economic group had not yet been separated from the religious group.

The Impermeability of Collective Durations

But the question of the separate character of these groups then arises. It is conceivable not only that these groups borrow a great deal from one another but also that their lives are intertwined, that these lines of evolution continually intersect. How is it possible to speak of many times if several currents of collective thought intermingle (at least periodically) in this way, exchanging substance and flowing through the same channel? Wouldn't they fix some remembrances in the same time? Tracing the evolution of a group—a religious group, for instance—through a given period, we see that contact with other groups is reflected in its thoughts. In *Port-Royal*, Sainte-Beuve understood that much more deeply this unique religious movement, and discerned that much more clearly its secret impulse and inner originality, as he brought into his portrait more events and personages from other milieus, each marking as it were an additional point of contact between the concerns of these religious recluses and the world outside. Most religious events are directed, in some fashion, toward the secular world and have an effect on it. The conversation in certain families and social gatherings centers on other families, politics, and artistic matters, as if they have been infiltrated by and swept into the momentum of these external milieus. Don't labels like "old-fashioned" or "progressive," when applied to various types of groups, refer to influences of this sort? A noteworthy event, whatever its social origins, may serve as a reference point for a group, helping to define the various stages of its duration. Isn't this proof that boundaries drawn between various collective currents are arbitrary, since these currents interact too often to be really distinct from one another?

According to this view, if the same event can affect more than one collective consciousness simultaneously, then these consciousnesses are, at that moment, interrelated and unified by a common representation. But is it really the same event? Each consciousness may represent the event in its own way and may translate it into its own language. Both groups and events have a spatial dimension, and an event may be perceived by more than one group. But what counts is the way a group interprets an event, the meaning given to it. For more than one consciousness to attribute the same meaning to an event, there must have been a prior merger of the groups. But the original premise is that they are distinct. Indeed, it is hardly conceivable that two collective thoughts would interpenetrate to such a degree. Groups certainly do merge, but the product is a new consciousness, differing in scope and content from those of the groups that merged. If not, the fusion is in appearance only, the groups soon returning to what they once were. One people may conquer and assimilate another, then either becoming a new people or at least entering a new stage of existence. If the conquerors do not assimilate the conquered, each then preserves its own national consciousness and responds to the same events in a different manner. This is also true of religious and political groups within a society. If the Church is subjugated and politicized by the State, it becomes an organ of the latter and loses its religious character. The current of religious thought diminishes, taking sanctuary in that element of the Church resisting its extinction. When Church and State are separate, the same event (the Reformation, for example) generates different representations in political and religious leaders. These different interpretations follow quite naturally from the distinct thoughts and traditions of the two groups.

Similarly, if the publication of Pascal's *Lettres provinciales* marks an important date in the history of literature as well as in the life of Port-Royal, this does not mean that the currents of literary and religious thought merged that year. Pascal didn't reconcile Montaigne and de Sacy, and the Jansenists continued to condemn the concupiscence of the mind. They considered Pascal only an instrument of God and probably attached more importance to his having been favored in his family by the miracle of St. Epine than to his activities as a writer. When Sainte-Beuve portrays for us those who entered Port-Royal, we faithfully capture the dual character of each personality. Though each is still the same individual, the image the world keeps of each one is far different from that in the memory of the Jansenists. All this brilliance and talent are extinguished. The conversion of each marks an end for one society and a beginning for another, as if this event had two dates that could not be placed in the same time. Of course, an event like this, involving moral development, becomes somewhat complicated. For example, a religious group and such a family might be similarly affected if the family were itself very religious.

When Madame Périer recounts the life of her brother, she speaks of him as though he were a Jansenist saint. Similarly, discussions of a politically active family connect it with those milieus whose exclusive concern is politics. But as we look more closely, the presence or absence of a certain shade of meaning will reveal whether politics or religion has superseded considerations of kinship—in which case, of course, this family has ceased to be a family.

On occasion, Pascal's bedroom was transformed into a monk's cell or a chapel and Madame Roland's salon gatherings could not be distinguished from a club or council of Girondist ministers. In other instances the family may, by contrast, seize upon religious or political images and events to nourish its own life. Family members may bathe in the reflected glory of a member who has gained fame in either milieu. They may feel more or less close as a family depending on whether their beliefs and convictions in these matters further unify or divide them. But this can happen only if these elements of thought, seemingly related to external objectives and persons, are transformed into familial representations. That is, despite their apparent political or religious form, their substance becomes the responses of kinship, the interests and preferences of the home, siblings, and ancestors. Usually such transpositions, whatever their character, occur because the family has held and practiced these religious or political beliefs for a long time. The peasant says, "My God and my King," but he means, "My home and my family." How many differences of belief and conviction are not also disguised antagonisms between siblings or parents and children! Of course, concern for family may fade and parents be totally forgotten. We are then truly enmeshed in that external milieu, be it religious or political or, for that matter, scientific, artistic, or economic. Since we do converse about such matters with our family, however, we don't have to forget about these groups to think about our family.

Slowness and Rapidity of Social Process

If the various currents of collective thought never really interpenetrate and cannot maintain contact, it is difficult to say whether time flows faster for one than for another. How can we know the speed of time if we have no common measure and cannot conceive any way of determining one speed relative to another? Nevertheless, we hear it said that life flows, thought and feelings proceed, with a more rapid rhythm in certain milieus than elsewhere. Should we define the speed of time according to the number of events it encompasses? But time is something quite different, as I have stated, than a successive series of facts or a sum of differences. We are deluded when we imagine that more events or differences mean the same thing as a longer time. We forget that events divide time but do not fill it up. Those who multiply their work and leisure activities end up losing the concept of real time. They may even extinguish the very substance of time, which becomes so fragmented that it can no longer spread out or offer any solidity. Since the capacity of the human group to change is limited, the more changes within a twenty-four-hour period, the less important each becomes. The activities of stock exchanges and commercial and industrial firms, involving so many daily transactions, usually take on a mechanical character.

Their members are continually occupied with the same kinds of calculations. Years and even decades must normally pass before the accumulation of all these words and actions eventuates in an important change that permanently alters the memory of these milieus— that is, the image kept of their past. Amid these semiautomatic activities, the group recognizes a relatively even time flowing at a snail's pace.

In addition, we often speak of backward peoples who have evolved very slowly. Within a nation it is commonplace to contrast the rapid rhythm of city life to the small town, of industrial regions to rural areas. We ought not to forget that the groups compared have neither the same character nor the same occupational structure. Assuming villagers have less occasion to redirect their daily thoughts and activities, does it follow that time flows more slowly for them? The city dweller believes this is the case, but why? He pictures the village as a city with gradually decreasing activity. But a village is a village and can be compared only with other villages and not with some other kind of group. In the rural areas time is divided according to a structure of occupations that are governed, in turn, by the cycles of animal and plant life. We must wait until the wheat germinates, eggs are laid, offspring are born, and the cow fills with milk. No mechanism can accelerate these processes. Time is as it must be for such a group and for men whose thought has a pace fitting their needs and traditions. Of course, slack and rush periods occur, but these atypical periods affect the content and not the course of time. Villagers may be absorbed in their work, conversation, daydreams, reflections, or reminiscences or in watching passers-by or playing cards. When these become a way of life—habitual activities regulated by custom, each having an appropriate time and place—then time is as it has always been, neither too slow nor too fast. Conversely, a peasant transported to the city will be astonished by the accelerated rhythm of life. He may imagine that a single day, being more full, must also condense more time. He pictures the city as a hyperactive village, full of supercharged human beings whose thoughts and actions make him dizzy. But the city is a city, a milieu in which transportation, recreation, and mental processes are as mechanized as productive activities. Time is divided as it must be and is neither too slow nor too fast, since it conforms to the needs of urban life. The thoughts filling its time are more numerous, but shorter, so they are not so deeply rooted in the mind. For a thought gains solidity only if it lasts long enough.

How can we use a comparison of the numbers of conscious states to measure the speed of time in two groups, unless the thoughts and representations in question are of the same type? In reality, time can be said to flow faster or slower only when societies are compared; but the concept of rapidity applied to the course of time offers no definite meaning. By contrast, in the act of remembering, thought is remarkable in its ability to travel quickly over large intervals of time. The speed with which it goes back in time varies, not only among groups but also among the members of a group and in the individual himself at different moments. When looking for a distant remembrance, we are occasionally astonished at the agility of the mind hurdling across vast periods and (as if equipped with seven-league boots) hardly noticing the representations of the past that apparently fill in that interval.

The Impersonal Substance
of Enduring Groups

But why should we imagine that all these distant remembrances are there, awaiting us in the order of their original occurrence? If the only way into our past were via all these differing images, each of which corresponds to an event that has occurred but once, then our mind would never skip or even skim over them but would survey them one by one. In reality, the mind does not review each image (for whose existence there is no proof anyway). It anchors itself in time, the time of a given group, and seeks there to recover or, rather, to reconstitute its remembrances. Time alone can serve this function, but only to the extent we represent it as a continuous and unchanging medium, the same today as it was yesterday, so that we can retrieve the yesterday in the today. Time remains relatively fixed over an extended period only if it serves as the common framework for the thought of a group that itself remains the same during that period, retaining a similar structure and focusing its attention on the same things. So long as my thought goes back within a period of this type, it moves in a milieu whose elements are all interconnected: it descends into and explores various areas in a continuous movement, with no barrier to moving still further back. My thought recovers the various elements of such a milieu merely by moving within it. Of course, this time is not identical to the events that have occurred within it. But neither is it to be reduced, as I have shown, to a homogeneous and empty framework. The traces of past events and people are present insofar as they have answered, and still do answer, an interest or concern of the group.

When I speak of the individual making use of the group memory, it must be understood that this assistance does not imply the actual presence of group members. I continue under the influence of a group even though I am distant from it. I need only carry in mind whatever enables me to gain the group viewpoint, plunge into its milieu and time, and feel in its midst. This statement certainly requires further explication. I picture myself conversing about psychology with an old friend from college. We describe and analyze the personality of our teachers and friends. We both belong to that group composed of all our fellow students, but our personal relationship, which antedates our entry into college, has created a still more intimate community. I have not actually seen him for many years, but our little group has continued in thought at least. Were we to meet tomorrow, we would retain the same attitudes regarding one another that we had before we parted. But he died a few months ago, and our group is dissolved. I will never be with him again. I can no longer evoke him as a living person. When I now picture us in past conversation, how can I claim to evoke these remembrances by relying on the memory of our group, since that group no longer exists? But a group is not only, or even primarily, a collection of definite individuals. Its reality is not exhausted in an enumerable set of individuals who constitute the starting point for its reconstruction. On the contrary, what constitutes the essence of a group is an interest, a shared body of concerns and ideas. The latter must be sufficiently general and even impersonal to keep its meaning and importance for me when members drop out and others (similar, but nonetheless new) are substituted. This interest or body of ideas and concerns represents the group's stable and permanent element, although it may be particularized and reflected to a certain extent through the personalities of group members. I don't retrieve it by going to these members, but, rather, I start from this element to reconstruct their person. If I think about my friend, therefore, I put myself into a current of shared ideas that continues for me even if he is gone. All that is necessary is that the conditions that enable me to place myself there are present about me. Now, these conditions are preserved because our concerns were not foreign to mutual friends, at least in this respect. I recognize in them similar character and thoughts, as if they had been virtual members of our group.

Suppose that a relationship between two or more persons lacked this element of common impersonal thought. Two people might be passionately in love, with thoughts only for each other. "I love him because he is who he is" or "I love her for herself alone" are ways they might express the fact that no substitute is possible. As passion died down, there would be no other bond of unity to replace it. Each lover would forget the other or preserve only a vague remembrance. What is the basis here that would help recall how each had once experienced the other? Remembrances may survive separations or death, however, because some common thought is present in addition to the personal attachment—perhaps a topic of meditation, the beauty of natural surroundings, or a sense of the transience of time. This stable element would transform a merely emotional union of two people into a group. This persisting group thought evokes that close relationship, now long gone, and saves the image of the person from oblivion. Could Auguste Comte have evoked Clotilde de Vaux with such lifelike reality had their love never become spiritualized as a union within the religion of humanity? Thus we remember our parents because we love them and, more important, because they are our parents. Two friends don't forget one another, because friendship presumes a harmony of thought and common concerns.

In reality, some of our relationships with people are incorporated into larger groupings in which we no longer represent other members in a concrete way. These groupings tend to transform, nearly depersonalize, people as we know them. What is impersonal is also more stable. The time in which a group has lived is a semi-depersonalized medium. We can assign more than one event within it because each has a meaning in relation to the whole. We recover this meaning from the whole, which lasts because its reality is not identical with the particular and transient figures traversing it.

The Permanence and Transformation of Groups: The Stages of the Family

Moreover, this permanence of social time is entirely relative. Our hold on the past, although it extends quite far in the various directions that interest group thought, remains limited. It never exceeds a certain boundary, which itself shifts as the groups to which we belong enter a new phase of their existence. It is as if the memory needed to be unburdened of the growing mass of events that it must retain. It is not the number of remembrances that matters. So long as the group has not visibly changed, the time embraced by its memory can lengthen, for it remains a continuous milieu accessible throughout. A new time emerges, however, as the group is transformed and turns away from what it no longer is. But the older time can exist alongside of, and even within, the new time for those members least affected by such a change. It is as if the older group refused to be totally absorbed into the new group born of its own substance. Memory thus reaches varying distances into a remote past, depending on what part of the social body is under consideration, because each organizes its thought about a differing center of interests and not because one has more remembrances than another.

The memory of a mother and father reaches back to that period between their marriage and their children's becoming conscious of the family milieu, about which the children know only what they are told. Is the family memory, then, no more than a conglomeration of individual sequences of remembrances? These sequences would be similar for that major portion of time when all members experienced the same events, but would end at different points in the family's past. Since the memory of each member may not extend equally into the past, are there then as many memories and as many perspectives on the same group as family members? Not at all, but we must acknowledge characteristic transformations in group life.

Some time passes between marriage and the moment when children become capable of remembering. These few years are filled with events, even though they may have seemed uneventful. The spouses discover not only the personal character of their partner but also how much they are the product of their own families and the other milieus in which they had lived. A new group can be built on these materials only by a great mutual effort full of surprises, difficulty, conflict, and sacrifice, as well as compromise, harmony, encouragement, and shared discoveries about society and nature. It is time devoted to laying the foundations of the house, times more vivid and endearing than the subsequent period of finishing the building. There is an excitement, a mutually shared vital impulse, present and working, for this is, in the first place, a beginning. Later on, efforts will have to be tailored to what has already been accomplished, as aspirations are balanced against responsibilities. The house must fit the neighborhood, and the needs of unanticipated inhabitants must be taken into account. The result is mishaps, lost time, and occasional readjustments. Work may even halt for one reason or another. There are unfinished houses and tasks that must wait before they can be resumed. *Pendent opera interrupta*—"The progress of the works remains interrupted" (Vergil). There is also the boredom of returning to work day in and day out at the same location. The completion of the edifice often evokes uneasiness rather than joy in its builders. Demolition evokes the specter of nature on the rampage, while workers laying the foundations resemble pioneers. How could the period when the bases of a new group are laid out not be filled with the most intense thoughts, destined to endure the longest of all? Thus the spirit of the founders survives in many societies, no matter how short the time devoted to laying the foundation.

The coming of children not only enlarges the family but often alters its thought and interests. The child is always an intruder in the sense that it will not adapt to the family, that the parents (as well as any previous children) must accept, if not every demand of the new baby, at least the changes resulting from its presence in the group. Up to this point the childless couple imagines itself self-sufficient. Its apparent independence arises from exposure to many external influences, such as reading, plays, travel, friends, and the husband's, and perhaps the wife's, occupation. The couple develops definite responses as it experiences these new milieus, gradually gaining awareness of its unity. It must weave its way between two dangers. Were it to retire within its own shell, abandoning even the contact that reading permits with external groups, it would be condemned to wither away, for it can live only from the social substance. Hence it always aspires to expand beyond the circle of its members. However, the equally risky alternative is to expand too far, to be absorbed by some external group or eccentric preoccupation. Especially in the beginning, therefore, the household may alternate between seeking and avoiding participation in society. This phase of such pronounced contrasts becomes set apart from all that will follow and deeply engraved in memory.

Later on the family establishes its place. It has its friends, interests, and social position. Its relationships with other groups are quite stable. Its essential concerns have taken on definite shape. A household with children understandably multiplies and specifies its relationships with the surrounding social milieu. More members, especially if they differ in age, mean that more facets of a group make contact with society. A family becomes more integrated into, and influenced by the spirit and rules of, the milieu of other families. A larger family might be thought a more self-sufficient and closed milieu, but this is not entirely true. The parents now have a common concern that is new and singularly powerful. But this more extended domestic group has more difficulty isolating itself physically and is more exposed to the views and opinions of others. The family consists of a totality of internal relationships, which grow more numerous, complex, and impersonal as it realizes in its own way the typical domestic structure of the external society. This transformation amounts almost to a new beginning, and family thought is profoundly altered in the process. This new phase constitutes the totality of family life for the children, for it is what they can remember. The memory of the parents goes back further, of course, because the group they once formed together has not been totally absorbed into the enlarged family. It has continued to live a sort of discontinuous and subdued existence. This becomes evident when the children grow up and leave. There is an atmosphere of unreality, akin to when two friends meet again after a long time. They can easily evoke a common past, but have nothing else to say to one another. It is as if they were at the end of a path that disappears or were players in a game whose rules they have forgotten.

Survivals from Extinct Groups

When a group or a society has undergone fundamental change, its memory seems to return to remembrances of the periods before and after that change via different pathways that are not continuous with one another. In reality, there are two times in which two frameworks of thought are preserved. The group must place itself within the one or the other to retrieve the remembrances localized there. How do we recognize the ancient city out of the labyrinth of new streets that have gradually encircled and disrupted it, out of the maze of homes and monuments that have either replaced or engulfed the buildings of now vanished neighborhoods? We don't go straight back into the past, pursuing in some reverse fashion the sequence of construction and demolition that has gradually altered the appearance of the city. To rediscover the old streets and edifices (whether still present or not), we have a general plan of the old city and are carried there mentally. For those who lived there before the city was enlarged and rebuilt, these segments of wall remain standing, and these building façades of another era and the sections of old road keep their former significance. We recognize characteristics of the old city in the modern city because we focus our thought and observation on this task. Similarly, those who knew a group before its transformation can, through the traces surviving from that past, provide access to another time and another past. Nearly every group in which we have spent some time leaves at least a trace of itself in later groups to which we belong. We can always penetrate into the time characteristic of a bygone group because these traces suffice to ensure the permanence and continuity of that time.

These coexisting times, even when they correspond to successive stages and forms of a society that has greatly evolved, remain in coexistence but are impermeable to one another. The groups to which they belong have a spatial and physical dimension, however, so group members can enter, simultaneously and successively, several of them. There is no unique and universal time, but society is broken into a multiplicity of groups, each having a characteristic duration. Collective times cannot be distinguished by their speed of flow. They cannot even be said to flow at all, since each collective consciousness is able to remember and the fixed character of time appears a necessary condition for memory. Events follow one another in time, but time itself is an immobile framework. Times are only more or less vast, permitting memory to go back varying distances into what is conventionally called the past.

Collective Durations as the Sole Basis of So-Called Individual Memory

Consider matters now from the point of view of the individual. He belongs to several groups, participates in several social thoughts, and is successively immersed in several collective times. The fact that people are not immersed, within a given time and space, in the same collective currents already permits an element of individual differentiation. Moreover, individuals vary in the speed at which and distance to which their thought goes into the past, or time, of each group. In this sense each consciousness may concentrate, in a given interval, durations of differing extent. That is, in a given interval of lived social duration, each consciousness is occupied with a varying extent of represented time. The range of variation, of course, is quite large.

A quite different interpretation is provided by those psychologists who believe that each individual consciousness has a distinctive duration, irreducible to any other. They consider each consciousness a flood of thought with its own characteristic movement. First of all, however, time does not flow, but endures and continues to exist. It must do so, for otherwise how could memory reascend the course of time? Moreover, how could a representation of time common to more than one consciousness be derived if each of these currents is a unique and continuous sequence of states that unfolds with varying speed? In reality, the thoughts and events of individual consciousnesses can be compared and relocated within a common time because inner duration dissolves into various currents whose source is the group. The individual consciousness is only a passageway for these currents, a point of intersection for collective times.

Curiously enough, philosophers of time have hardly considered this conception until recently. They have continued to picture the individual consciousness as isolated and sealed within itself. The expression "stream of thought," or psychological flux or current, found in the writings of William James and Henri Bergson, translates with the help of an appropriate metaphor the feeling that each of us experiences when he is a spectator at the unfolding of his own psychic life. It is as if, within each of us, our states of consciousness follow one another in a continuous current, like so many waves pushing one after another. This is indeed true, as reflection confirms, of thinking that continually progresses from one perception or emotion to another. By contrast, memory characteristically forces us to stop and momentarily turn aside from this flux, so that we might, if not reascend, at least cut across a current along which appear numerous branchings off, as it were. Of course, thought is still active in memory, shifting and moving about. But what is noteworthy is that only in this instance can it be said that thought shifts and moves about in time. Without memory and apart from those moments when we remember, how could we ever be aware of being in time and of transporting ourselves through duration? Absorbed in our impressions, pursuing them as they appear and then disappear, we doubtless merge into one moment of duration after another. But how can we also represent time itself, that temporal framework that encompasses many other moments as well as this one? We can *be* in time, in the present, which is a part of time, and nevertheless not be capable of *thinking* in time, of taking ourselves back in thought to the near or more distant past. In other words, we must distinguish the current of impressions from the current of thought (properly so called), or memory. The first is rigidly linked to the body, never causes us to go outside ourself, and provides no perspective on the past. The second has its origins and most of its course in the thought of the various groups to which we belong.

Suppose now that we focus on groups and their representations, conceiving individual thought as a sequence of successive viewpoints on the thought of these groups. Then we will understand how a person's thought can go varying distances into the past, depending on the extent of the perspectives on the past provided by each collective consciousness in which he participates. One condition is necessary for this to be the case. Past time (a certain image of time) has to exist immobile in each collective consciousness and endure within given limits, which vary by group. This is the great paradox. On reflection, however, we realize it could not be otherwise. How could any society or group exist and gain self-awareness if it could not survey a set of present and past events, if it did not have the capacity to reascend the course of time and pass continually over traces left behind of itself? Every group—be it religious, political or economic, family, friends, or acquaintances, even a transient gathering in a salon, auditorium, or street—immobilizes time in its own way and imposes on its members the illusion that, in a given duration of a constantly changing world, certain zones have acquired a relative stability and balance in which nothing essential is altered.

Of course, how far we may so return into the past depends on the group. Consequently, individual thought, depending on the degree of its participation in a given collective thought, attains ever more distant remembrances. Beyond this moving fringe of time or, more correctly, of collective times, there is nothing more, for the time of the philosophers is an empty form. Time is real only insofar as it has content—that is, insofar as it offers events as material for thought. It is limited and relative, but it is plainly real. Moreover, it is large and substantial enough to offer the individual consciousness a framework within which to arrange and retrieve its remembrances.

4. Space and the Collective Memory

The Group in Its Spatial Framework: The Influence of the Physical Surroundings

Auguste Comte remarked that mental equilibrium was, first and foremost, due to the fact that the physical objects of our daily contact change little or not at all, providing us with an image of permanence and stability. They give us a feeling of order and tranquility, like a silent and immobile society unconcerned with our own restlessness and changes of mood. In truth, much mental illness is accompanied by a breakdown of contact between thought and things, as it were, an inability to recognize familiar objects, so that the victim finds himself in a fluid and strange environment totally lacking familiar reference points. So true is it that our habitual images of the external world are inseparable from our self that this breakdown is not limited to the mentally ill. We ourselves may experience a similar period of uncertainty, as if we had left behind our whole personality, when we are obliged to move to novel surroundings and have not yet adapted to them.

More is involved than merely the discomfort accompanying a change of motor habits. Why does a person become attached to objects? Why does he wish that they would never change and could always keep him company? Let us leave aside for the moment any considerations of convenience or aesthetics. Our physical surroundings bear our and others' imprint. Our home—furniture and its arrangement, room décor—recalls family and friends whom we see frequently within this framework. If we live alone, that region of space permanently surrounding us reflects not merely what distinguishes us from everyone else. Our tastes and desires evidenced in the choice and arrangement of these objects are explained in large measure by the bonds attaching us to various groups. All we can say is that things are part of society. However, furniture, ornaments, pictures, utensils, and knick-knacks also "circulate" within the group: they are the topic of evaluations and comparisons, provide insights into new directions of fashion and taste, and recall for us older customs and social distinctions. In an antique shop the various eras and classes of a society come face to face in the scattered assortment of household belongings. One naturally wonders who would have owned such an armchair, tapestry, dishes, or other necessities. Simultaneously (it is basically the same thing), one thinks about the world recognizable in all this, as if the style of furniture, the manner of décor and arrangement, were some language to be interpreted. The picture a Balzac provides of a family lodging or the home of a miser, a Dickens gives of the study of a notary public, already suggests the social type or category of the humans who live in that framework. What is involved is no mere harmony and physical congruence between place and person. Rather, each object appropriately placed in the whole recalls a way of life common to many men. To analyze its various facets is like dissecting a thought compounded of the contributions of many groups.

Indeed, the forms of surrounding objects certainly possess such a significance. They do stand about us a mute and motionless society. While they do not speak, we nevertheless understand them because they have a meaning easily interpreted. And they are motionless only in appearance, for social preference and habits change; for example, when we grow tired of a piece of furniture or a room, the object itself seems to age. In truth, the impression of immobility does predominate for rather long periods, a fact explained both by the inert character of physical objects and by the relative stability of social groups. It would be an exaggeration to maintain that changes of location and major alterations in the furnishing demarcate stages of family history. However, the permanence and interior appearance of a home impose on the group a comforting image of its own continuity. Years of routine have flowed through a framework so uniform as to make it difficult to distinguish one year after another. We doubt that so much time has passed and that we have changed so much. The group not only transforms the space into which it has been inserted, but also yields and adapts to its physical surroundings. It becomes enclosed within the framework it has built. The group's image of its external milieu and its stable relationships with this environment becomes paramount in the idea it forms of itself, permeating every element of its consciousness, moderating and governing its evolution. This image of surrounding objects shares their inertia. It is the group, not the isolated individual but the individual as a group member, that is subject in this manner to material nature and shares its fixity. Although one may think otherwise, the reason members of a group remain united, even after scattering and finding nothing in their new physical surroundings to recall the home they have left, is that they think of the old home and its layout. Even after the priests and nuns of Port-Royal were expelled, nothing was really affected so long as the buildings of the abbey stood and those who remembered them had not died.

Thus we understand why spatial images play so important a role in the collective memory. The place a group occupies is not like a blackboard, where one may write and erase figures at will. No image of a blackboard can recall what was once written there. The board could not care less what has been written on it before, and new figures may be freely added. But place and group have each received the imprint of the other. Therefore every phase of the group can be translated into spatial terms, and its residence is but the juncture of all these terms. Each aspect, each detail, of this place has a meaning intelligent only to members of the group, for each portion of its space corresponds to various and different aspects of the structure and life of their society, at least of what is most stable in it. Of course, extraordinary events are also fitted within this spatial framework, because they occasion in the group a more intense awareness of its past and present, the bonds attaching it to physical locale gaining greater clarity in the very moment of their destruction. But a truly major event always results in an alteration of the relationship of the group to place. The family as a group may change size owing to death or marriage, or it may change location as it grows richer or poorer or as the father is transferred or changes occupation. From then on, neither the group nor the collective memory remains the same, but neither have the physical surroundings.

The Stones of the City

The districts within a city and the homes within a district have as fixed a location as any tree, rock, hill, or field. Hence the urban group has no impression of change so long as streets and buildings remain the same. Few social formations are at once more stable and better guaranteed permanence. Paris and Rome, for example, have seemingly traversed the centuries without rupturing the continuity of life, despite wars, revolutions, and great crises. The nation may be prone to the most violent upheavals. The citizen goes out, reads the news, and mingles with groups discussing what has happened. The young must hurriedly defend the frontier. The government levies heavy taxes that must be paid. Some inhabitants attack others, and political struggle ensues that reverberates throughout the country. But all these troubles take place in a familiar setting that appears totally unaffected. Might it not be the contrast between the impassive stones and such disturbances that convinces people that, after all, nothing has been lost, for walls and homes remain standing? Rather, the inhabitants pay disproportionate attention to what I have called the material aspect of the city. The great majority may well be more sensitive to a certain street being torn up, or a certain building or home being razed, than to the gravest national, political, or religious events. That is why great upheavals may severely shake society without altering the appearance of the city. Their effects are blunted as they filter down to those people who are closer to the stones than to men—the shoemaker in his shop; the artisan at his bench; the merchant in his store; the people in the market; the walker strolling about the streets, idling at the wharf, or visiting the garden terraces; the children playing on the corner; the old man enjoying the sunny wall or sitting on a stone bench; the beggar squatting by a city landmark. Not only homes and walls persist through the centuries, but also that whole portion of the group in continuous contact with them, its life merged with things. This part of the group is just not interested in what is happening outside its own narrow circle and beyond its immediate horizon. The passivity that the group sees in this portion of itself that remains unconcerned about the passions, hopes, and fears of the outside world reinforces that impression arising from the immobility of things. The same is true for disturbances in smaller groups based on blood, friendship, or love when death, disagreements, or the play of passion and interest intervene. Under the shock of such troubles, we walk the streets and we are surprised to find life going on about us as if nothing had happened. Joyful faces appear at windows, peasants converse at the crossroads, buyers and sellers stand on shop steps, while we, our family, our friends, experience the hurricane of catastrophe. We, and those whom we hold dear, constitute only a few units in this multitude. Doubtless any one of these people I meet, taken aside and put back into his own family or group of friends, would be capable of sympathizing with me as I described to him my troubles and concerns. But people, be they in a crowd or scattered about in mutual avoidance of one another, are caught up in the current of the street and resemble so many material particles, which, packed together or in movement, obey laws of inert nature. Their apparent insensitivity is wrongly condemned by us as something like nature's indifference, for even as it insults us, it momentarily calms and steadies us.

The best way of understanding the influence the physical environment of the city exerts on groups that have slowly adapted to it is to observe certain areas of a modern metropolis: for example, the older districts, or the relatively isolated sections that form little self-enclosed worlds where the inhabitants live very near their work, or even the streets and boulevards in the newer parts of the city peopled primarily by workers, where a great deal of human traffic occurs between lodging and street and neighborhood relationships multiply. But it is in the smaller cities lying outside the mainstream of modern life, or in Oriental cities (where life is still regulated with a tempo such as our cities had one or two centuries ago), that local traditions are most stable. There the urban group really constitutes (as it does elsewhere only in part) a social body with subdivisions and a structure reproducing the physical configuration of the city enclosing it. The differentiation of a city arises from a diversity of functions and customs. Whereas the group evolves, the external appearance of the city changes more slowly. Habits related to a specific physical setting resist the forces tending to change them. This resistance best indicates to what extent the collective memory of these groups is based on spatial images. Cities are indeed transformed in the course of history. Entire districts may be left in ruins following siege, occupation, and sacking by an invading army. Great fires lay waste whole areas. Old homes deteriorate. Streets once inhabited by the rich change appearance as they are taken over by the poor. Public works and new roads require much demolition and construction as one plan is superimposed on another. Suburbs growing on the outskirts are annexed. The center of the city shifts. Although older districts, encircled by newer and taller buildings, seem to perpetuate the life of former times, they convey only an image of decay, and were their former inhabitants to return, it is doubtful that they would even recognize them.

Were the relationship between streets, homes, and groups inhabiting them wholly accidental and of short duration, then men might tear down their homes, district, and city, only to rebuild another on the same site according to a different set of plans. But even if stones are movable, relationships established between stones and men are not so easily altered. When a group has lived a long time in a place adapted to its habits, its thoughts as well as its movements are in turn ordered by the succession of images from these external objects.

Now suppose these houses and streets are demolished or their appearance and layout are altered. The stones and other materials will not object, but the groups will. This resistance, if not in the stones themselves, at least arises out of their long-standing relationships with these groups. Of course, this arrangement was work of an earlier group, and what one group has done may be undone by another. But the design made by the original people was embodied in a material structure. The force of local tradition comes forth from this physical object, which serves as its image. This shows the extent to which a whole aspect of the group imitates the passivity of inert matter.

Implacement and Displacement: The Adherence of the Group to Its Location

This resistance can emanate only from a group. There is no mistaking this point. Urban changes—the demolition of a home, for example—inevitably affect the habits of a few people, perplexing and troubling them. The blind man gropes for his favorite spot to await passers-by, while the stroller misses the avenue of trees where he went for a breath of fresh air and is saddened by the loss of this picturesque setting. Any inhabitant for whom these old walls, run-down homes, and obscure passageways create a little universe, who has many remembrances fastened to these images now obliterated forever, feels a whole part of himself dying with these things and regrets they could not last at least for his lifetime. Such individual sorrow and malaise is without effect, for it does not affect the collectivity. In contrast, a group does not stop with a mere display of its unhappiness, a momentary burst of indignation and protest. It resists with all the force of its traditions, which have effect. It searches out and partially succeeds in recovering its former equilibrium amid novel circumstances. It endeavors to hold firm or reshape itself in a district or on a street that is no longer ready-made for it but was once its own. For a long time old aristocratic families and long-standing urban patriarchs did not willingly abandon the districts where they had resided from time immemorial. Despite their growing isolation, they refused to move into the new neighborhoods of the wealthy, with their broader streets, nearby parks, open spaces, modernistic style, and activity. The poor also resist, often aggressively, their dislocation and, even in submission, leave behind a good deal of themselves. Behind the new façade, and on the outskirts of avenues lined with the recently built homes of the wealthy, the public life of the common people in the past takes shelter in the malls, alleys, and lanes, only to recede gradually—hence those little islands out of the past that we are surprised to find in the midst of fairly modern districts. In totally remodeled districts, contrary to our expectations, we find that houses of entertainment, small theaters, unofficial money-changers and secondhand stores curiously reappear after a time. This is especially true of certain crafts, small businesses, and similar types of activity that are old-fashioned and no longer suited to the modern city. These activities are driven by an impulse acquired in the past and would quickly die if removed from their traditional locations. Certain small businesses are well patronized because, from time immemorial, they have been located at a site that marks them for public attention. There are old hotels, dating from the time of stagecoaches, that continue to be used simply because they are in a memorable location. All these routines and remnants from the past require some sort of collective automatism for their explanation, an enduring rigidity in the thought of certain relationships of businessman and customer. These groups adapt slowly, and in many circumstances demonstrate an extraordinary capacity not to adapt. They long ago designed their boundaries and defined their reactions in relation to a specific configuration of the physical environment. The walls against which they have built their shops, the material framework enclosing them, and the roofs sheltering them have become integral parts of the group. To lose their location in the pocket of a certain street, or in the shadow of some wall or church, would be to lose the support of the tradition that recommends them and gives them their unique reason for existence. Hence we can understand why the remains of demolished buildings or roads persist for a long time, be it only the traditional name of a street or locale or the signboard of a store.

Groups Without an Apparent Spatial Basis: Legal, Economic, and Religious Groups

The groups we have discussed up to this point are connected naturally to a certain place because spatial proximity has created social relationships between members. Hence a family or household can be externally defined as a set of persons living in the same house or apartment—as the census puts it, "under the same lock and key." The inhabitants of a town or district form a small society because they are together in the same area. It goes without saying that this is not the only condition necessary for the existence of such groups, although it is an obvious and essential one. Indeed, this condition is less important for the vast majority of social formations, which tend to detach people from space by emphasizing characteristics other than residence. The bonds of kinship encompass more than merely living under the same roof, and urban society is something more than a mass of individuals living alongside one another. Legal relationships are based on individuals having rights and being able to contract obligations independently of their physical location (at least in the Western world). Economic groups are based on positions in production, not space, on the diversity of occupations, types of remuneration, and distribution of goods. Economically speaking, people are defined and compared on characteristics of person and not place. This is even more true for religious groups. They establish invisible bonds between their members and emphasize the inner man. Each of these groups is superimposed on localized groups. Indeed they subdivide the latter according to rules that take no account of spatial configuration. Therefore, the fact that men live in the same place and remember its image never suffices for the discovery and recollection of the group to which they belong.

Nonetheless, in briefly reviewing the most important collective formations that are different from the localized groups previously studied, we see that it is difficult to describe them if we avoid all spatial imagery. That difficulty increases as one goes further into the past. We may say that legal groups can be defined by their members' rights and obligations. But we know that the serf was formerly bound to the soil, that the only way for him to escape servitude was to join an urban community. A man's legal condition, then, was a result of where he lived, country or city. Moreover, the legal system governing the land varied and the city charters did not grant the same privileges. The Middle Ages, it is said, was a particularistic age. There were many regimes, each associated with a specific locale, so that to know a man's habitation was tantamount, for others and himself, to knowing his legal status. The functioning of justice and the tax system in premodern times cannot even be described without detailed knowledge of the territorial subdivisions. Each province (in England, each county) and each city had its own time-honored legal system and particular customs. In England the royal tribunals gradually supplanted the courts of the manor, while in France, after the Revolution, every citizen was made equal before the law and for tax purposes. We have our present uniformity because the various regions of the country no longer represent so many distinct legal systems. Making the laws uniform, however, could not by itself standardize the varying conditions of the land or situations of the individual. Law must in its applications disregard local circumstances. But collective thought is bound to these very circumstances and thus finds the law irrelevant. Hence the countryside still attributes some legal significance to different spatial situations. In the mind of a rural commissioner or village mayor, meadows, fields, woods, farms, homes, all evoke property rights, sales contracts, easements, mortgages, leases, land patterns—that is, a whole series of legal actions and situations that a simple image of this land as it appears to a stranger would not contain, but that are superimposed on it in the legal memory of the peasant group. These remembrances are connected with different parts of the land. They mutually reinforce one another because the parcels of land to which they relate are side by side. These remembrances are preserved in group thought because they are founded on the land, because the image of the land endures outside them and may be recaptured at any moment.

Indeed every transaction and commitment in the countryside involves land. But in the city, law covers other matters using other material frameworks. Here also the notary public or auctioneer, in handling a person's interests or effecting for him a transfer of rights, has as a normal consideration the material things. Once the client has left his office or the auction is completed, these objects may leave the area and never be seen again. Yet the notary will recall the real estate he has sold, settled in dowry, or bequeathed. The auctioneer will remember an exceptional price bid at the sale of a certain piece of furniture or work of art that he will never see again, as both belong to types of objects that he thinks about and sees continually in his work.

It is different for service transactions and bank or stock exchange operations. A worker's labor, a clerk's skills, a doctor's medical concerns, a lawyer's legal aid, are not objects which occupy a definite and stable spatial location. We never situate credits and debts, or the values of titles or copyrights, in a place. This is the world of money and financial transaction, where specific objects, bought and sold, are unimportant and what matters is the capacity to acquire or dispose of anything. Nevertheless, services are rendered and tasks are executed, and their value for the purchaser depends on their being performed in a specific office or factory. A union secretary or labor mediator passing by a factory or picturing its location has an image that is only a part of a more extensive spatial framework comprising every factory whose workers and management concern him. This framework enables him to remember various kinds of wage contracts, conflicts over them, as well as all the laws, rules, and customs (local or occupational) that define the situation and the respective rights of workers and employers. Financial and banking activities are placed within a spatial framework of the institutions where we must go to sign papers and withdraw or deposit funds. Of course, the picture of a bank recalls only a few specific activities or, rather, a sequence of vaguely understood procedures. But this is all that ordinarily occupies that type of memory that barely extends into the past. Notary public, mayor, auctioneer, union secretary, and labor mediator have been selected as examples because their memory has to acquire the greatest scope and clarity for legal relationships and actions connected with their occupations. They represent the focus of a memory that is itself collective, extending over every group concerned with that particular legal matter. Showing that this memory, for those who best embody it, is based on an image of a certain place proves that the same is true for all members. Various objects and their spatial arrangement have a meaning related to the rights and obligations connected with them, and group members are enclosed within a distinct world of legal relationships formed in the past but continually present to them.

Similar reasoning applies to many other types of groups. For example, we no more need to visit the country to learn that a farm is both a place of habitation and work than we need to walk the streets of an ancient city and read signs saying "Tanners Street" or "Goldsmiths Street" to recall a time when occupations were grouped by location. In modern society, home and place of work are clearly separate. The equipment and men performing the tasks are brought together daily in the factories, offices, and shops. Clearly such small economic groupings are formed on a spatial basis. Similarly, in large cities districts are distinguished by the predominance of a certain occupation or industry or by varying degrees of poverty or wealth. These social variations are obvious to the casual observer, and almost every part of the urban landscape bears the imprint of one social class or another.

Similarly, religions are rooted in the land, not merely because men and groups must live on land but because the community of believers distributes its richest ideas and images throughout space. There are the holy places and other spots that evoke religious remembrances, as well as the profane sites inhabited by enemies of God, which may even be cursed and where eyes and ears must be closed. Nowadays, in an old church or convent, we inattentively walk on flagstones marking the location of tombs and don't even try to decipher the inscriptions engraved in the stones on the sanctuary floor or walls. Such inscriptions were continually before the eyes of those who worshipped in this church or belonged to this convent. The space that surrounded the faithful was permeated with religious meaning by means of funeral stones, as well as altars, statues, and pictures of the saints. We fashion a well-nigh inaccurate conception of the way their memory arranged remembrances of ceremonies and prayers, of all the actions and thoughts that make up the devout life, if we are ignorant of the fact that each found its place in a specific location.

The Insertion of the Collective Memory into Space

Thus, every collective memory unfolds within a spatial framework. Now space is a reality that endures: since our impressions rush by, one after another, and leave nothing behind in the mind, we can understand how we recapture the past only by understanding how it is, in effect, preserved by our physical surroundings. It is to space—the space we occupy, traverse, have continual access to, or can at any time reconstruct in thought and imagination—that we must turn our attention. Our thought must focus on it if this or that category of remembrances is to reappear.

While it might be conceded that every group and every kind of collective activity is linked to a specific place, or segment of space, it could be argued that this fact alone is quite insufficient to explain how the image of a place conjures up thoughts about an activity of the group associated with that place. While each mental picture does have a framework, there is no strict and necessary relationship between the two; the framework cannot evoke the picture. Such an objection would be valid if the term "space" referred solely to physical space—that is, the totality of forms and colors as we perceive them about us. But is that how we originally experience space? Is that normally how we perceive the external milieu? It is difficult to know just what space would be like for a genuinely isolated man who had never belonged to any society. Let us speculate as to what conditions are necessary if we are to perceive only the physical and sensory qualities of things. We must divest objects of many relationships that intrude into our thought and correspond to a like number of different viewpoints. That is, we must dissociate ourselves from any group that establishes certain relationships between objects and considers them from given viewpoints. Moreover, we would succeed in doing so only by adopting the attitude of another group, perhaps that of physicists if we claim to focus our attention on certain abstract properties of matter, or that of artists if we concentrate on line and shading of figures and landscapes. Back on the riverbank, at the park entrance, or amid the activity of the street after a visit to an art gallery, we still feel that impulse from the society of painters, as we view things not as they really are but as they appear to one trying only to reproduce an image of them. Actually, nothing is less natural. Of course, remembrances of interest to other groups cannot find a place to be preserved in the space of the scientist or painter, since it is constructed by the very elimination of all other spaces. But this does not prove that these other spaces are less real than those of the scientist or painter.

Legal Space and the Memory of Laws

Legal space is not an empty milieu merely symbolizing a still undefined possible world of legal relationships among men. Were it so, there would be no way a given part of it could evoke one specific relationship rather than another. Consider the law of property, which is basic to all legal thought and is a possible model and starting point for defining every other obligation. It results from society's having adopted an enduring attitude toward a certain piece of land or a physical object. Whereas land is fixed and physical objects, if not fixed, retain their properties and appearance, so that in both cases identity through time is assured, human beings may change location as well as inclination, capacity, or effort. An individual or several individuals acquire property rights only when their society grants the existence of a permanent relationship between them and an object, one as immediate as the object itself. Such a convention does violence to reality, for individuals are constantly changing. Any principle invoked as a basis for property rights gains value only if the collective memory steps in to guarantee its application. Suppose I were the first person to occupy or clear a certain piece of land, or that a certain possession is the result of my own labor. If we can't go back to the past, and if there is a dispute about the original situation that could undermine my claims, how would I verify the original state of affairs unless the group preserved a remembrance of it? But the memory guaranteeing the permanence of such a situation is itself based on the permanence of space, or at least on the permanence of the attitude adopted by the group toward this part of space. Things, and the signs and symbols that society attaches to them, that are always in its thoughts as it focuses on the external world, must be considered together as a totality. These signs are not external to things, related only artificially and arbitrarily to them. The Magna Carta, drawn up following the conquest of England, registered on paper not the division of lands but the power exercised on it by the various barons to whom it was distributed. Similarly, in the case of a land registry or other legal certificate recalling the existence of some property right, society not only establishes a relationship between the image of a place and a document but considers that place as already linked to that person who has posted or fenced it, resided there continually, or cultivated it for his own benefit. Everything of this type can be called legal space—a permanent space (at least within certain time limits) allowing the collective memory at any moment to recover the remembrance of legal rights at issue there.

Thought concerning the rights of persons over things considers not only the relationship between man and things but also man himself as permanent and unchanging. Of course, in a peasant community, the rights evoked in a notary public's office or before a judicial tribunal clearly relate to specific persons. But thought, insofar as it focuses on the legal aspect of facts, preserves the person only in his relevant characteristic as holder of a recognized or disputed right, as owner, usufructuary donatory, heir, and so forth. Whereas a person normally changes from one moment to another, as a legal entity he never does. Law talks much about "will"—for example, about the will of the parties concerned—but this term refers only to intentions resulting from the legal character of the person, deemed the same for every person with this legal character and unchanging as long as the legal situation remains unchanged. This tendency to disregard individual characteristics when considering a person as having rights explains two fictions consistent with the legal mentality. When a person dies leaving a natural heir, it is said that "death lays hold of life"—that is, everything continues as if there had been no interruption in the exercise of rights but a continuity between the persons of the heir and the deceased owner. Again, several individuals joined together to acquire and manage possessions are assumed to form a group having a legal personality that is unchanging so long as the contract of association remains, even when every original member has left and been replaced by someone else. Hence persons endure because things do, and legal proceedings concerning a will may carry on for many years, with a definitive judgment reached only after the allotted years for a human life have passed. The memory of the legal society will never be at fault so long as the goods themselves remain.

Property rights, however, are exercised not only over land or specific objects. In modern society liquid wealth has greatly increased and (far from remaining stationary in location or form) circulates continuously outside our notice. Everything boils down to commitments contracted between lenders or creditors and borrowers or debtors. But the object of the contract occupies no fixed location, for it pertains to money or debts—that is, abstract signs. Moreover, other obligations may have no reference to things at all but give one party rights over the services, acts, or even the absence of such of the other party. Again, where only persons are in a relationship and goods are no longer at issue, space would seem to be left out of the picture. Nevertheless, every contract, even if possessions are not involved, places two parties in a situation deemed unchanging so long as the contract remains valid. Here we have a fiction introduced by society, which considers the parties bound together once the clauses of the contract are settled on. But it is impossible that the stability of individuals and the permanence of their reciprocal attitudes would not be expressed in a material form nor take shape in space. At all times each party must know where to find the other as well as the boundaries of their powers with regard to the other. The most extreme form of a person's power over another is the law that once gave one possession of slaves. In truth, a slave was only a person reduced to the state of a thing. There was no contract between master and slave, and property law treated the latter like any other possession. Slaves nonetheless were still men and, unlike things, could injure their master's rights by claiming free status on the basis of false documents, running away, or committing suicide. That is why the slave had a legal status, though it conferred only obligations and no rights. In ancient homes, slaves' quarters were separated from the master's, where they might enter only when ordered. Such a separation of space into two parts was enough to perpetuate in the minds of master and slave the image of the former's unlimited rights over the latter. Far from his master's sight, the slave could forget his servile condition, but on entering the master's area he once again became aware of being a slave. It was as if crossing that threshold transported him into a region of space where the very remembrances of his subjection to the master were preserved.

Neither slavery—or, for that matter, serfdom—nor the different estates of noble, commoner, and so forth are still with us. We now accept only those obligations we ourselves have contracted. Nevertheless, consider a worker or clerk summoned into his employer's office or about a debtor entering a commercial house or bank from which he had borrowed and to which he now comes, not to pay off his debt, but to secure an extension or even to borrow more. Perhaps they too have forgotten the service or money they owe. If they do recall them, and if they suddenly find themselves in a subordinate situation, it is because the residence or usual location of the employer or creditor represents for them an active zone, a focal point radiating the rights and powers of one free within limits to affect their person. The circumstances and meaning of the contract they have signed seems to be reconstituted and evoked anew in their memory as they enter this zone or approach this focal point. Of course, these instances are exceptional. A person may well be in a position of both superiority and subordination to another. Thus, Mr. Smith, a commoner, may have a gentleman of the gentry as a debtor, but not dare to claim what is rightfully his. What is essential is that every contract specify either the place where it must be executed or the residence of each party, so that the creditor knows where he can reach the debtor and the debtor knows the source of the instructions he receives. Moreover, these zones, in which one person feels himself master, another subordinate, really come down to some localized area—for example, the place each party lives or the boundaries of the factory—so that as soon as a person enters the factory or place of business he feels the pressure of the rights that another has over him. Occasionally this pressure extends even further, and the insolvent debtor, subject to bodily seizure, may not even dare go out on the streets.

At this point, however, law and breach of the law are involved, not merely a contract between two individuals. Ordinarily we think about our obligations regarding public order only when we do, or are tempted to, violate them. Then there is hardly any part of space occupied by the society that has made those laws where we do not feel ill at ease, as if we fear to incur repression or censure. But even when we are within the law, legal thought is still there, extended over the ground. The ancients never separated their picture of the city from the remembrance of its laws. Even today, when we travel from our own country to a foreign one, we have a very distinct feeling of passing from one legal zone into another, for the line separating them is physically marked on the ground.

Economic Space

Economic life relates man and material goods, but in a different way from the exercise of property rights or the making of contracts pertaining to things. We leave the world of law to enter the world of value. Although both of these worlds differ greatly from the physical world, we may very well be further removed from the latter when we evaluate objects than when we determine in accord with our fellow men the extent and limits of our rights over parts of the material world.

However, we talk about prices, not values, because prices, after all, are what we work with. Prices are attached to things like so many labels, for there is no relationship between an object's physical appearance and its price. It would be otherwise if the price a person paid, or were ready to pay, for a thing answered his desire or need for it. Likewise, it would be so if the price he asked measured his pain and sacrifice either for giving up this possession or for working to replace it. If either condition were the case, there would be no point in speaking of an economic memory; each person would evaluate objects with regard to his momentary needs and his actual feeling of pain in producing or being deprived of them. But such is not the case. Instead, we know that people evaluate objects—the satisfactions they bring as well as the effort and work they represent—according to their price; and prices are set up outside ourselves, in our economic group. Now, to so assign a price to an object, a person must somehow have reference to the reigning opinions of his group regarding its utility and the amount of work it requires. But this opinion, in its present state, is primarily explained by its prior state, today's price by yesterday's. Economic life, therefore, is based on the memory of previous prices and, at the very least, of the last price. Buyers and sellers—that is, group members—refer to them. But these remembrances are superimposed on the immediate objects by a series of social decrees. Now, then, can the mere appearance and spatial position of these objects suffice to evoke such remembrances? Prices are numbers representing measures. Whereas numbers corresponding to physical properties are, in a certain sense, in the objects (since they can be rediscovered by observation and measurement), here in the economic world material objects acquire a value only from the moment a price is assigned them. This price has, therefore, no relationship with the object's appearance or physical properties. How could the image of the object possibly evoke the remembrance of its price—that is, a sum of money—if the object is represented to us as it appears in physical space and hence separated from all connection with group life?

Precisely because prices result from social opinions dependent on group thought and not from the physical properties of objects, the place where these opinions concerning the value of things are formed and where the remembrances of prices are transmitted is able to serve as the basis of the economic memory, instead of the space occupied by the objects. In other words, in collective thought certain parts of space are differentiated from all others to serve as the ordinary gathering places of groups whose function is to recall for themselves and other groups the prices of various products. The remembrances of exchange activities and the value of objects—that is, the whole content of memory of the economic group—is normally evoked within the spatial framework made up of these places.

Simiand once spoke of a shepherd in the mountains who, having given a traveler a bowl of milk, did not know what price to charge him and so inquired: "What would you have been charged in the city?" Likewise, peasants who sell eggs and butter determine their price by the price at the last market. Such remembrance, first and foremost, refers to a period very near in time, as do almost all remembrances stemming from the market or economic opinion. Indeed, if the aspects of production ascribable to technique (with which I am not at present concerned) are left aside, the conditions of buying and selling, prices, and wages will be found to undergo continued fluctuation. In no sphere do the latest remembrances more quickly and completely banish earlier ones. Of course, the rhythm of economic life may vary. When manufacturing procedures changed very slowly in the times of the guilds and small industry, buyers and sellers experienced long periods of price stability and were subjected to only very mild fluctuations. But the situation changed when the technology and needs were transformed simultaneously, in a competitive economic system enlarged to the borders of the nation and beyond. The price system, much more complex than before, experiences severe fluctuations, which spread from one region or industry to another. In having to continually readjust to the new conditions of equilibrium, buyers and sellers forget older habits, intentions, and experiences. Merely consider those periods of rapid inflation, when money plummets in value as prices uninterruptedly increase, and we must fix a new standard of values in mind from one day to the next, even from morning to evening. Such drastic differences can also be observed, at a given moment or within a given period, between distinct spheres of economic life. Peasants go to the market or the city once in a long while, so they may well imagine that prices have not changed since their last transactions. They live on their remembrance of past prices. This is not the case in those milieus where contacts between merchant and customer are more frequent. In particular, among those circles of wholesalers and retailers who buy not solely to satisfy their own consumption needs or sell not merely to dispose of products, but who buy and sell as "middlemen" between consumers and producers, the economic memory must take account of and fix the most recent relationships and prices. This is even more true of stock exchanges, where prices of securities change not only from day to day but from hour to hour during a session, since all the forces altering the opinions of buyers and seller are immediately felt and since the only way of guessing or predicting what prices will be is to buy at the latest quotation. As one moves away from these circles of most intense exchange activity, the economic memory slows down, bases itself on an older past, and falls behind the present. It is the merchants who give it new impetus and force renewal.

Merchants, then, teach and remind their customers of current prices. Buyers as such participate in the life and memory of the economic group only on entering merchant social circles or when recalling to mind previous contacts. Enclosed within the family and separated from currents of exchange as they are, is there any other way they could know the value of goods and evaluate in monetary terms what they use? Let us take a closer look at these merchant groups, which, as I have stated, make up the most active part of economic society, since within them values are generated and conserved. Congregated in stands at the marketplace or set side by side on a city's commercial streets, merchants might at first seem opposed to one another rather than joined together by a sort of common consciousness. Their relationships are with customers. As sellers, they dissociate themselves from neighboring merchants, whom as competitors they pretend to ignore or who simply sell another kind of goods. Even though lacking direct communication, they are all agents of a single collective function. They bear a similar mentality, evince typical aptitudes, and obey a common occupational ethics. Although competitors, they sense their solidarity when it is a matter of maintaining price levels and passing them on to the customer. Most important of all, they are all linked to wholesaler groups and, through them, to both the commercial stock exchanges and to banking circles and big business, that part of economic society where most information is concentrated, which immediately reflects the repercussions from commerical dealings and has the most effective role in the determination of prices. The latter is the regulatory organ through which all the merchants are linked to one another, since the sales of each merchant affect its reactions and, in turn, obey its impulses. Thus, retail merchants represent the contours and limits of an economic society whose center and heart are the stock exchange and banking circles, while contact between these poles is maintained by traveling salesmen, brokers, and advertising and information agents.

The customer-consumer is not included in this whole set of activities. The merchant's counter is like a screen that prevents the customer's peering into those areas where prices are formulated. This is more than mere metaphor. We shall see that the merchant group is thus spatially immobilized and fixed in given places to wait on the customer, because only then can he fulfill his function in economic society. Now let us look at things from the customer's point of view. As stated, customers can learn to evaluate consumer goods only if merchants let them know the prices. Hence they must come to the merchant, for it is a necessary condition of exchange that the customer know where he can find him. (At least, this is generally the case, although we must remember the peddler who does selling door to door—an exception that only proves the rule, as we shall see.) Merchants therefore wait in their shops for customers.

Not only the merchant but at the same time the merchandise awaits customers. This statement constitutes not two expressions of the same fact but two distinct facts that must be considered simultaneously because each of them, as well as their relationship, enters into the economic representation of space. In effect, because the merchandise waits—that is, stays in the same place—the merchant is forced to wait—that is, to stick by a fixed price (at least for the duration of a single sale). The customer is actually encouraged to make a purchase on the basis of this condition, because he gets the impression of paying for the object at its own price, as if the price resulted from the very nature of the object, rather than at a price determined by a complex play of continually changing evaluations. Of course, this impression is an illusion because the price is attached to the thing just as a price tag is to a specific article, for it is constantly changing while the object is not. Even though a customer may bargain, seemingly taking account of whatever is fictitious in the determination of price, in reality he remains convinced there is a true price corresponding to the thing's value. The merchant is either concealing this true price and the customer is trying to make him acknowledge it, or the merchant is stating the true price and the customer is trying to make him forget it. The merchant endeavors to persuade the buyer that the object is being sold at its own price and to avoid giving the idea that the price comes from outside and is not in the object. But he manages to establish, only gradually, a fixed price for an object by offering it at the same price over some varying length of time.

Anyone buying furniture, clothing, or even merchandise for immediate use may well imagine that it keeps its value, as measured by the price paid the merchant, the entire time it is used. Such a belief would often be in error, for were he to resell the item, either immediately or later on, or have to replace it, he would find that its price had changed. The buyer lives on old remembrances. The remembrances of the merchant regarding prices are more recent because, selling to many people, he disposes of and must reorder articles more quickly than any buyer might repurchase any item from him. Nevertheless, he is in the same position in relation to his wholesaler as the customer is to him. Hence retail prices change more slowly than wholesale prices. This, then, is the retailer's role: he must stabilize prices enough to allow customers to make purchases. His role is only a particular application of a function fulfilled by the whole society. Although everything is continually changing, society must persuade its members that it is not changing, at least in certain aspects over a given period. Likewise, the society of merchants must persuade customers that prices are not changing, at least during the time necessary for them to make a decision. It succeeds only on the condition that it stabilize and fix itself in certain places to await customers. In other words, prices can be fixed in the memory of buyers and even sellers only if they simultaneously think about the places where goods are sold as well as the goods. The economic group cannot extend its memory sufficiently, or project its remembrances of price into a distant enough past, unless it endures—that is, remains unchanged in the same locations. Members re-establish the world of values, for which these places serve as a continuous framework, by resituating themselves, in fact or in thought, at the locations.

Religious Space

Religious groups may recall certain remembrances on viewing specific locations, buildings, or objects. This should be no surprise, for the basic separation between the sacred and the profane made by such groups is realized materially in space. The believer entering a church, cemetery, or other consecration place knows he will recover a mental state he has experienced many times. Together with fellow believers he will re-establish, in addition to their visible community, a common thought and remembrance formed and maintained there through the ages. Of course, many of the faithful live virtuously in the secular world, in occupations unrelated to religion and amid social milieus with quite different purposes, and never forget to relate to God as much as possible of their thought and action. Religion permeated the ancient city, and in very old societies—China, for example—hardly any area escaped the influence of supernatural forces. The size and number of spaces consecrated to religion or habitually occupied by religious communities declines, however, as the major activities of social life are separated from the grip of religion. "For the saint all is saintly," and no place is so profane that a Christian cannot evoke God there. The faithful nevertheless experience a need to congregate periodically in buildings and at sites consecrated to holiness. Entering a church does not suffice to recall to us in a detailed and precise manner our relationships with the group holding similar beliefs. But we find ourselves in that mental disposition common to the faithful when gathered in a place of worship—something that has to do not with events as such but with a certain uniform bent of thought and sensibility. This certainly provides the most important basis and content of the religious collective memory. There is no doubt of its preservation at consecrated areas, for as soon as we return to such areas, we recover it.

We may even imagine that the group memory endures much like the buildings presumed to house it and that a single current of religious thoughts has uninterruptedly flowed beneath the roofs of such holy places. Certainly the church is empty at times, doors locked and walls sealing in only lifeless objects. The group is dispersed at such moments, but it endures and remains what it has been; when the group comes together again, there would be no reason to assume it has changed or had even ceased to exist so long as the faithful could pass by the church, view it from afar, or hear the bells, so long as they could hold in mind or readily evoke the image of their congregating together and the ceremonies they have participated in behind these walls. But, on the other hand, how can they be sure that their religious feelings have not changed and remain today what they were yesterday, that past and present remain indistinguishable in those feelings, unless the very permanence of physical location carries that guarantee? A religious group, more than any other, needs the support of some object, of some enduring part of reality, because it claims to be unchanging while every other institution and custom is being modified, when ideas and experiences are being transformed; whereas other groups are satisfied to persuade members that rules and arrangements remain the same during some limited period, the religious group cannot acknowledge that it differs now from what it was in the beginning or that it will change in the future. Since the world of thought and feeling fails to provide the requisite stability, it must guarantee its equilibrium through physical things and in given areas of space.

The church is not merely a place where the faithful congregate, an enclosure protected from the influences of the profane. First, its interior appearance distinguishes it from every other gathering place or center of collective life. Its arrangement reflects devotional needs and is inspired by the traditions and thoughts of the religious group. The layout of the church, because its various parts are prepared for different kinds of worshipers and because the essential sacraments and principle forms of devotion are especially suited to particular locations, demands of members a certain physical distribution and bodily posture as it deeply engraves in their minds images that become fixed and immutable as the rituals, prayers, and dogmas. Religious practices unquestionably require that certain areas of a church be separate from the rest. Group thought needs such focal points for its attention—places to project, as it were, a major portion of its substance. Also, the priests are knowledged in the traditions, so that every detail of interior arrangement has meaning and corresponds to a particular orientation of religious thought, whereas the masses of faithful usually gain but an impression of mystery from these material images. Hence, in ancient temples—in Jerusalem, for example—not all the faithful were admitted into the most sacred areas, the sanctuary and the Holy of Holies. A church is like a book whose printed characters are understandable only to the very few. As the group attends services and receives instruction within such buildings, its thoughts are profoundly shaped by these physical objects. Finding images of God, apostles, and saints everywhere, surrounded by lights, ornaments, and ecclesiastical vestments, the faithful picture the sacred beings, heaven, and the transcendental truths of dogma in such a framework. Hence religion is expressed in symbolic forms that unfold and cohere in space. This condition alone guarantees its continued existence. That is why the altars of the ancient gods must be over-turned, and their temples destroyed, if remembrances of a more primitive worship are to be obliterated from the memory of men. Scattered and distant from their sanctuaries, the faithful lament their condition and feel their god has abandoned them, whereas each time a new church is raised, the religous group feels that it grows and grows stronger.

But every religion also has a history. Rather, there is a religious memory composed of traditions going back to events, often very far in the past, that occurred in definite locations. It may well be difficult to evoke the event if we do not think about the place itself. Yet in most cases, we are acquainted with this place not because we have seen it but because we know that it exists and could be seen. At any rate, its existence is guaranteed by the testimony of witnesses. That is why there is a religious geography or topography. The Crusaders, arriving at Jerusalem to retake possession of the holy places, were not satisfied to seek out the places where the principal events of the Gospels were traditionally situated. Very often they localized, more or less arbitrarily, various details from the life of Christ or the early Christian Church, guided only by unreliable vestiges and, in their absence, by momentary inspiration. As many pilgrims came to pray at these places, new traditions were elaborated. Today it is difficult to distinguish those remembrances of places going back to the early centuries of the Christian era from everything the religious imagination has since added. Of course, all these localizations are accepted on faith, for none had been warranted by a tradition of sufficient antiquity and continuity. Moreover, several traditions were attached to the same place at one time. For example, we know that more than one of these remembrances obviously erred in locating the Mount of Olives and that Mount Zion was shifted from one district to another. We know that certain remembrances have attracted others or, conversely, been divided up—the repentance of Peter, for example, being separated from the denial and fixed at another location. If the Church and the faithful tolerate these variations and contradictions, is this not evidence that the religious memory needs to imagine places in order to evoke the events connected with them? Of course, not every believer can make a pilgrimage to Jerusalem and contemplate with his own eyes the holy places. But it is enough to picture them and know they continue to exist, and about the latter they have no doubts.

Moreover (leaving aside the role that the belief in holy places has played in the history of Christianity as well as other religions), there is something exceptional about religious space: God being present everywhere, every area is capable of participating in the sacred character of these privileged sites where He once manifested Himself. The faithful need only wish collectively to commemorate at a given site some act or personal aspect of God, in order that such remembrances become connected with this location, enabling the remembrances themselves to be recovered. As we have seen, any church building can function in this way. The crucifixion not only occurred on Golgotha but also occurs whenever we adore the cross, and Jesus not only shared communion with his disciples in the Cenacle but does so wherever Mass is celebrated and the faithful receive the Eucharist. Other examples could include the chapels consecrated to the Virgin, apostles, and saints, as well as the many places with their ancient relics, healing springs, or tomb sites where miracles occurred. Of course, commemorated places are more numerous in Jerusalem, Palestine, and Galilee: a whole evangelic history is written on their soil. These regions are doubly consecrated, not only by the will and faith of succeeding generations of pilgrims but also because here, in the time of Christ, it is believed that one could have seen all that is recounted in the holy books. However, since the invisible and eternal meaning of these facts is of primary importance, any place may serve so long as the same attitude is adopted—that is, so long as the cross and sanctuaries so prominent in the historical theater of the Gospels have been reproduced in a material form. Thus arose the devotion of the "stations of the cross," as if the believer, by re-enacting far from Jerusalem the episodes of the Via Dolorosa, would be in a position to relive inwardly, just as pilgrims do, the successive episodes of the Passion of our Lord. In any case, the end pursued is always the same. The religious society must persuade itself that it has not changed, even when everything about it is in transformation. It succeeds only by recovering places or by reconstructing about itself an image (at least a symbolic one) of those places in which it originated. Since places participate in the stability of material things themselves, some similar procedure is a primary condition of memory itself: the collective thought of the group of believers has the best chance of immobilizing itself and enduring when it concentrates on places, sealing itself within their confines and molding its character to theirs.

Summary

Summarizing our discussion, we may say that most groups—not merely those resulting from the physical distribution of members within the boundaries of a city, house, or apartment, but many other types also—engrave their form in some way upon the soil and retrieve their collective remembrances within the spatial framework thus defined. In other words, there are as many ways of representing space as there are groups. We may focus our attention on the limits of ownership, such as the rights associated with various parts of the land, and distinguish between locations occupied by master and slave, lord and vassal, noble and commoner, creditor and debtor, as active and passive zones respectively, from which radiate and on which rights are given or removed from a person. We may consider the locations of economic goods, goods that acquire a value only when offered for sale in the marketplace or shop—that is, at the boundary separating the economic group of sellers from their customers. Here again, one part of space is differentiated from the rest—namely, where the most active part of society interested in goods ordinarily resides and leaves its imprint. Finally, we may be most sensitive to that separation between sacred and profane places that is paramount in the religious consciousness. For there are certain areas of space that the faithful have chosen, "forbidden" to anyone else, where they find both shelter and support for their traditions. Hence each group cuts up space in order to compose, either definitively or in accordance with a set method, a fixed framework within which to enclose and retrieve its remembrances.

Now let us close our eyes and, turning within ourselves, go back along the course of time to the furthest point at which our thought still holds clear remembrances of scenes and people. Never do we go outside space. We find ourselves not within an indeterminate space but rather in areas we know or might very easily localize, since they still belong to our present material milieu. I have made great efforts to erase that spatial context, in order to hold alone to the feelings I then experienced and the thought I then entertained. Feelings and reflections, like all other events, have to be resituated in some place where I have resided or passed by and which is still in existence. Let us endeavor to go back further. When we reach that period when we are unable to represent places to ourselves, even in a confused manner, we have arrived at the regions of our past inaccessible to memory. That we remember only by transporting ourselves outside space is therefore incorrect. Indeed, quite the contrary, it is the spatial image alone that, by reason of its stability, gives us an illusion of not having changed through time and of retrieving the past in the present. But that's how memory is defined. Space alone is stable enough to endure without growing old or losing any of its parts.

5. The Collective Memory of Musicians

The remembrance of a word always corresponds to an external model or schema that is fixed either in the phonetic usage of a group (that is, in an organic support) or in the printed form (that is, on a material surface). In this way it differs from the remembrance of any other sound, natural or musical: most human beings, on hearing sounds that are not words, have no way of comparing them with models purely auditory in character, simply because they lack such models.

When I raise my head in my study and listen for a moment to the sounds within and without, I can certainly state that, for instance, this noise is the coal shovel in the hallway; that, the step of a horse in the street; the other, the cry of a child. But evidently, such similar categories of sounds or noises are not ordinarily grouped about some symbolic auditory representation. When I wish to recognize these sounds, I think about objects or beings that, to my knowledge, produce similar sounds; that is, I refer to conceptions not essentially sonorous in character. The sound makes one think about the object because the object is recognized through the sound; but only rarely might the object (the model to which one refers) itself evoke the sound. On hearing the clinking of chains, one might think of a prison gang; or the jingling of bridles, the cracking of a whip, and the galloping of horses might remind one of a chariot race. Were such scenes to appear on a movie screen without a hidden orchestra accompanying and imitating these sounds, we would not evoke them on our own and the figures moving in silence would present a much less effective illusion.

But it is no different when a human voice is involved, as our attention focuses no longer on the words as such but on timbre, intonation, and accent. Suppose that in the darkness or on a telephone we were to hear speaking, in turn, a person we know and a person we do not know. Hearing a person without seeing him, we can think only about his voice. But what does that voice make us think about? Rarely do we refer to an auditory model, as though our primary interest were an analysis of the character of these voices and their potential effect on the public's ear, a viewpoint perhaps paramount in conservatory examinations or to a theater director. On hearing a familiar voice we tend to think of persons we recognize, while on hearing an unknown voice we consider instead the character and feelings expressly or apparently revealed. Hence we refer to certain familiar ideas and reflections, laden not only with images of parents and friends but also with images representing sweetness, tenderness, coldness, maliciousness, bitterness, and deceit. We confront the voices we have heard with these conceptions, as stable as our conceptions of objects, so that we might recognize the voices or be placed in a position of recognizing them. Thus, we are occasionally suprised to come upon a total stranger who speaks just like a parent or friend—surprised and perhaps humored, for it is as if our parent had put on a mask, or as if the stranger were wrong to assume a voice not belonging to him. Something similiar also occurs when the intensity of vocal utterances is totally at variance with physical appearance—as, for example, when a man of slight build speaks with a deep bass voice.

We come now to musical sounds. Were we limited to hearing musical sounds in order to fix them in memory and be able to recall them, most notes or musical sound combinations that strike our ears would be quickly lost. Berlioz recounted in his memoirs that one night he composed a symphony in his head that he considered excellent. He was going to write it out on paper when it occurred to him that to perform the symphony would cost him much time and money, so he decided to abandon it and write nothing. The next morning, he could remember nothing of what he had created and had heard within himself with such clearness only a few hours earlier. How much truer this must be for those of us who have learned neither to sight-read nor to perform. On leaving a concert, we retain in memory almost nothing of a piece just heard for the first time. The melodic themes break up and notes scatter like pearls from a necklace whose thread has broken. Of course, we may be able to recognize and recall this or that tune, theme, melody, sequence of notes, or even harmonies and portions of a symphony, although we are ignorant of musical transcription. Such cases may involve something that we have heard several times and learned to reproduce vocally. Musical sounds are not fixed in memory as auditory remembrances; instead, we learn to reproduce a sequence of vocal movements. In so retrieving a tune, we refer to one of these active motor schema that Bergson speaks about. While fixed in our brain, such schemas remain outside consciousness. Or such instances could merely entail sequences of sound that we are incapable of producing on our own but can recognize when they are executed by someone else (and only then).

Suppose, then, that we recognize a tune played on a violin as one we had previously heard played on a piano. Where is the model to which we refer? It must be both in our brain and in sonorous space. The model is in our brain as an acquired capability to reproduce what we have already heard—an inadequate and incomplete capability, however, since we cannot reproduce the tune on our own. The sounds we now hear encounter these crude movements of reproduction. Thus what we recognize is something in these sounds that matches these movements: not timbre but, essentially, varying pitches of sound, pauses, and rhythms, that part of music that can actually be transcribed and pictured in visual symbols. Of course, we hear other things. We hear the sounds themselves, the sounds of the violin, so different from that of the piano, the music played on the violin, so different from the same tune played on the piano.

Nevertheless, we recognize this tune because, without reading notes or seeing them written on a sheet, we imagine in our own way these symbols that direct the musician's movements, symbols that are the same whether played on the piano or on the violin. Therefore, there would be no recognition, and memory would retain nothing, were there no movements in the brain and no notes conveyed by musicians.

We have distinguished in our preceding discussion two ways by which people who know neither how to read music nor how to play an instrument might recall a musical theme. Some recall it because they can reproduce it in song. Others, because they have already heard it and are able to recognize certain passages. Let us now consider two additional ways of recalling a musical theme, ones limited, however, to musicians and to people who know how to read music. The former recall music because they can play it; the latter, because they have read beforehand or are currently reading the score and recognize the music as they hear it performed. The exact same relationship holds between these types of musicians, those who play and those who are imagining the sequence of musical symbols as they listen, as holds between those who can sing a tune and those who recognize it by ear, although neither of the latter two know how to read music. The musical memory in the group of musicians is naturally more extensive and far more reliable. Let us as external observers study a bit more closely its apparent mechanism.

Imagine an orchestra in a concert hall: each member is playing his part, eyes fixed on a piece of paper on which marks are printed, These marks represent notes, their pitch, beat, and the intervals separating them. It is as if there were so many signals on that sheet showing the musician what he must do. These are not images of sounds that might reproduce the sounds themselves. No natural relationship exists between the marks and notations read by the eye and the sounds heard by the ear. The marks and notations do not represent sounds because there is no resemblance between the two. But they translate into conventional language a whole series of commands the musician must obey if he wishes to reproduce any sequence of notes with the proper nuance and suitable rhythm.

But what does the musician actually see when he looks at these sheets? The number of marks that strike his retina decreases or increases, just as it does for any kind of reading, depending on the reader's proficiency. Differentiate between the marks themselves and the combinations into which they may enter. The marks are limited in number and relatively simple in character. Admittedly, as a result of reading them and performing the instructions so transmitted, the musician has wholly assimilated their meaning: the marks have been in some sense or another inscribed in his brain and no longer need be seen to be recalled. By contrast, the possible combinations of marks is infinite, and some are so complex as to defy the belief that all these combinations are conserved in the cerebral matter as mechanisms that might prepare the movements necessary to reproduce them.

In any case, this is unnecessary, for these combinations of marks are inscribed outside the brain on sheets of paper—that is, physically preserved. Barring certain very exceptional cases, the brain of the musician neither contains nor preserves, in any form sufficient for reproduction, the score of every piece of music he has ever played. Generally speaking, even performing a rehearsed piece, the musician does not know it by heart, as he needs from time to time to look at the score. Had he not assimilated beforehand the basic marks and even their most frequent combinations, he would be in a situation similar to that of a person reading out loud who must continually stop because of letters he does not recognize. He would have to learn the music by heart in order to play in an orchestra or in public; he would no longer need a score but would have much more work before each performance and be quite limited in the number of pieces he would be in a position to perform. The elementary musical marks and their combinations reside in his brain; it is quite useless to preserve also complex combinations, which it suffices to have on sheets of paper. Thus the score in this case functions exactly as a material substitute for the brain.

Consider the attitudes and actions of musicians in an orchestra. Each musician is only one part of a whole that includes the other musicians and a conductor. They play in time and with harmony: often each member knows not only his own part but the others' parts also, as well as the relationship of his to theirs. This whole also includes the written scores. As in any organism, there is a division of labor, different functions executed by different organs; and if the motor centers determining the musician's movements are considered to be in the brain or the body, then it might be said that the visual centers are partly outside the brain or body, since the musician's movements in this case are linked to the notations read off the scores.

This description, recognizably enough, only approximates reality. Indeed, some musicians could perform their whole part by heart. Others, even though following the scores with their eyes, still know whole sections by heart. Depending on the personal capacity of the musician, his degree of training, and amount of rehearsal, he will be able to a greater or lesser degree to dispense with the external support that the printed or written marks offer his memory. But, no matter what his degree of virtuosity, he could never retain every work that he has played so as to be able to reproduce it at will at any time. At any rate, isolate the musician and deprive him of all these means of translation and fixation of sounds that musical script represents: he would find it quite difficult, if not almost impossible, to fix so many remembrances in his memory.

Musical characters and the cerebral alterations that correspond to them are artificial and differ, therefore, from sounds and the traces left in our brain by sounds. Musical symbolism is conventional and has meaning only for the group who has invented or adopted it. Consider a physiologist who is totally ignorant of music, who knows nothing of concerts, orchestras, or musicians. Were he able to penetrate the musician's brain, he would perceive movements occurring there and connect them to their external causes, knowing with certainty that some were due to these natural physical phenomena called sounds. But by observing this brain while the musician is reading a score as he performs, the physiologist would distinguish, alongside the cerebral traces of sounds, other traces connected to these printed characters. All he could say about them is that they are not encountered in nature.

He might well experience the astonishment of a Robinson Crusoe exploring his island and sighting in the sand, not far from the sea, footsteps. Suppose these tracks had been left by men whom he had not seen come the previous day and who had since departed. Many other kinds of traces would still remain—i.e., animal tracks, bird feathers, sea shells. Human footsteps, however, differ from these other traces that are present on the island as the result of nature at work. The island, so to speak, produced them by itself. Thus, as he broods over the tracks, Robinson really sees something that is no longer his island. Even though imprinted in the sand, these footprints convey him elsewhere. Through them he resumes contact with the world of men, since these footprints have meaning only if restored to the totality of "tracks" left on the earth by the activities of men in groups. The same holds true for these traces left in the cerebral matter by musical characters: they reveal the action exerted on the human brain by what a physiologist might call a system or colony of other human brains.

This type of action is peculiar in that it works by means of characters; that is, it assumes a prior and continuous agreement among men regarding the meaning of these characters. These cerebral changes, although occurring in several brains, nonetheless constitute one whole in their exacting interrelationship. Furthermore, the symbol as well as the instrument of this unity, of the unity of this whole, exists materially—namely, the musical characters and the printed sheets of the score. Whatever occurs in the brain due to this agreement and this unity cannot be considered in isolation.

For someone ignorant of the musician's group, the action exerted on his brain by these musical signs would be trivial, evaluated as it would be solely in terms of the sensory properties of the signs themselves. Such properties scarcely differentiate this sign from the many other objects in sight that exert no action on the musician. This perception of a musical character will gain its full value only when replaced within the totality to which it belongs: that is, the remembrance of a sheet covered with notes is but a part of a larger remembrance or a body of remembrances. As one sees the score in one's mind, one also glimpses a whole social milieu—the musicians, their conventions, and the obligation imposed on them to comply with these conventions in order to establish a suitable relationship.

Let us turn once again to the musicians playing in an orchestra. Their eyes are fixed on their scores; their thoughts and movements are in harmony, being but so many copies of a single model. Assume that all the musicians have memorized sufficient amounts to be able to play without casting more than an occasional glance. The scores are still present, but they might as well not be. Nothing would change were they absent, since the musicians' thoughts are in accord and the scores have no other role than to symbolize this agreement of thoughts. Could it not, therefore, be said that there is no reason to explain the conservation of musical remembrances in terms of the scores—the memory needing the support of an enduring material object—precisely because the scores cease to play a role as soon as the remembrance has been acquired? In stating that the musicians and their scores formed a totality that must be considered part of any explanation of the preservation of remembrances, have I not placed myself at that moment when the remembrance does not yet exist and is still in the process of formation? If so, does the score, the external material object, not simply lose all its importance as soon as the remembrance exists and the musician can evoke it at will? Consequently, we should revert to a purely physiological theory of the memory. That is, we should acknowledge that the brain suffices to account for the recall and recognition of these remembrances.

Nonetheless, in my opinion, the musician playing by heart differs only in degree from his fellow musician reading the notes on a stand. Note that before he plays by heart, he must first have read and reread his part. Whatever the time between that last reading and the performance—be it hours, days, or even longer—the nature of the action, which the system of characters exercises on the musician who translates it, has not changed. Every sensation requires a certain time period for us to become aware of it, since there is never immediate contact between consciousness and object. The sensation usually originates and exists at a time when the object itself is no longer present. Will it be said, therefore, that the object is not the cause of the sensation? As I have stated elsewhere, there are grounds for distinguishing active memory, which functions to recall or recognize for us an object no longer acting on us, from resonance, the delayed and continuing action that an object still exerts on our mind even though a time interval of varying length has lapsed since we first perceived the object. Hence the object need no longer be present, but if the action that it exerts continues, the system that the representation and the object form is nonetheless a continuous circuit sealed by the object, however remote in time that may be. In our instance, the object is a set of characters. The action that it exerts is the instructions conveyed to the subject. The musician no longer reads the score, but he behaves as if he were. The musical signs have not passed from the score to his mind as so many visual images, for he no longer sees them. Will it be said that the movements he performs are connected, that a mechanism has been set up in his brain, so that each movement automatically determines the following one? Certainly. But what must be explained is precisely how this mechanism has been set up. It must be related to its cause, which is external to the musician; and this cause is the system of signs put on paper by the group.

Consider a tablet of wax engraved with a series of letters and words. Its grooves reproduce the characters on the stamp. The stamp has since been thrown away. Its imprint remains, and it might be thought that these characters, left behind, are connected in such a manner that each word is explained by the one preceding. We know this is not so, that the waxen imprint is the result of a stamp, that the action of the stamp continues to exist unchanged in nature even though its characters are no longer applied to the impressions. Similarly, a man may find himself part of a group in which he learns to use certain words in a certain way. He may then go far from this group, but so long as he still uses this language, the action of the group can still be said to be exerting itself on him. There is no more an interruption between individual and group in this case than there is between a painting and the hands and thoughts of the painter who composed it some time ago. Such also is the relationship between the musician and a sheet of music that he has read, perhaps reread several times, although he now apparently can do without it. Far from being able to dispense with the sheet music, in reality he can only play because it is there, invisible yet all the more active, just as one is never better obeyed than when one's orders are carried out without having to repeat them.

We can now state where the model is that allows us to recognize the pieces of music we do remember. We have emphasized our present topic because musical remembrances are infinitely diverse and certainly, as the psychologist would say, part of the domain of pure quality. Each theme, each phrase, each section of a sonata or symphony, is unique unto itself. In the absence of any system of notation, a person wishing to memorize everything a musician must play for a series of concerts would seemingly have to line up one after another the impressions for all the moments. What kind of infinitely complex characteristics would have to be attributed to a brain to enable it to record and preserve separately so many representations and images?

According to Bergson, however, this need not be the case. We need only refer to some schematic model in which each piece of music heard has been replaced with a series of signs. We need no longer retain separately each successive sound, unique in its own right (as I have noted), but only a small number of notes equal to the number of musical signs. Obviously, the various methods of combining these sounds must be retained, and there are many—as many as there are pieces—and each is distinct. But these complex combinations break down into simpler combinations. Though these simpler combinations still exceed the number of notes, they often recur within a single piece or are found in other pieces. An accomplished musician, who has played many different selections, would be like a prolific reader. Words are more numerous than letters; combinations of words, than words themselves. What is new on each page is neither the words nor even the parts of the phrases, all of which are rather rapidly retained. What must be retained or understood, what must be the focus of attention, is the combination of elementary themes, the collection of (already known) notes or words. Thus the task of the memory is reduced and simplified. A person could learn by heart whole pieces, even a great many pieces and, on hearing one, recognize the entire sequence of notes as it unfolds. He need only keep somehow in mind a model schematically representing how these familiar terms enter into new modes of combination. All that need be represented is a collection of signs.

But what is the source of these signs? How does this schematic model itself arise? Assume Bergson's viewpoint, which has to do with an isolated individaul. This man hears the same piece of music many times. Each hearing corresponds to an original sequence of impressions that is not confused with any previous one. But each hearing produces in his cerebrospinal system a sequence of motor reactions that is reinforced, always in the same direction, from one hearing to the next. These reactions end up designing a motor schema. This schema constitutes the fixed model with which we afterward compare the piece as it is heard and that enables us to recognize and even to reproduce it. In this matter Bergson accepts the physiologic theory of memory, which explains this type of recall and recognition as a function solely of the individual brain.

Of course, individuals with an equally "good" ear react differently to a rendition of the same piece (no matter how often repeated), depending on whether or not they know how to sight-read music. But this is a mere difference of degree. A musician who has studied a piece before hearing it has broken it down. He has focused on the elements, represented by notes. First he has isolated the various motor reactions corresponding to each note. Such movements stand out because of their greater frequency. Then he has practiced combining these movements according to the combinations of notes he hears and reads. He now has a precise understanding of the movements, since he knows their exact composition. What is so surprising about the fact that he can immediately represent this collection of movements with the help of signs? A person who has never paid attention to the elementary reactions in himself determining solitary sounds, let alone simple combinations of sounds, will have much more difficulty distinguishing the movements he carries out when hearing a piece of music. These movements will be more confused and less precise. Usually, they will remain as rather rudimentary motor movements. But they are not in essence different from those of a musician. What proves this is the fact that a person who has never studied music nevertheless manages to recall certain themes, either because he has heard them quite often or because he has made special note of them for one reason or another.

According to Bergson, therefore, a musical sign's function is not indispensable. Quite the contrary, musical signs emerge only after we distinguish elementary notes. But what is given would be a set of sounds blended together—i.e., a whole continuum. We must first of all break this down; that is, our nervous system must respond to each sound or elementary collection of sounds with a distinct reaction. Then we can represent these separate movements by signs. Brain movements are then transformed into signs, and not the signs into brain movements. Moreover, to go back from the notes to the movements is a natural operation, since the notes are merely the translation of these movements. But the movements would come first, as the text precedes the translation.

Nonetheless, there is one fact that this explanation leaves unanswered, no doubt because it does not emerge into plain view when man is considered in isolation. In point of fact, these signs result from collective agreement. Musical language is a language like any other; that is, it presupposes a prior agreement among those who "speak" it. In order to learn any language, we must undergo an arduous training that substitutes for our natural and instinctive reactions, a series of mechanisms whose model is found completely outside ourselves, in society.

In the case of musical language, the matter might be thought to be quite different. There does exist a science of sound based on natural data from physics and physiology. Let us grant that the cerebral and nervous system of man may be a resonating apparatus, naturally capable of recording and reproducing sounds. Musical language would then be limited to stabilizing, through signs, the movements of these mechanisms when placed in a milieu of sound. The convention that we discussed would thus be based on nature, for all intents and purposes existing in its entirety just as soon as one of these mechanisms has been set up. But to reason in this manner is to forget that adults and even children, before learning about music, have already acquired many habits. In other words, these mechanisms have already been functioning for a long time. Their movements differ not only in degree, as if some were more sonorous than others, or as if their corresponding notes were more distinct. The notes are different or, rather, are combined differently. The difficulty consists precisely in ensuring that these mechanisms become, or become once again, one and the same, their parts moving in the same way. This can happen only by starting with a model independent of any single mechanism.

The music of the musicians is not the only kind. From an early age, the baby is reared on the songs of his nurse. Later he repeats the tunes that his parents hum. There are songs for play as there are songs for work. Popular songs pass from mouth to mouth in city streets, once reproduced by organ grinders and today by phonographs. The monotonous chants of wandering merchants, the melodies of the dance, fill the air with diverse sounds and harmonies. People don't have to study music to preserve remembrances of tunes and songs. But are they musicians for all that? Were there only a difference of degree between the person who recognizes a tune because he has heard it often and the musician who recognizes it because he has read or is reading it from a score, we might also believe it sufficient to fill the memory with tunes and songs in order to be able to learn music quite easily; and a very modest additional effort would gain for us the knowledge of the written notes of these sounds we have heard and repeated. This, however, is just not true. Someone familiar with many tunes must still have a complete musical education to be able to sight-read them. He must devote just as much time and effort as a person who has heard and retained only a few tunes. Moreover, he may well have more difficulty assimilating musical language, since his original vocal habits may not so easily disappear. In other words, these two ways of learning to retain sounds, the popular and the academic, have no relation to one another.

How do we recall a tune if we are not a musician? Consider what is the most elementary and probably the most frequent case.

On hearing a song with words, a person distinguishes as many parts as there are words or phrases. The sounds seem connected to the words, which are discontinuous objects. Words here play the active role. However, one can often reproduce a tune without thought to the accompanying words. The tune does not evoke the words. By contrast, it is difficult to repeat the words of a familiar song without inwardly singing it. In the first case, moreover, the words are probably present when we reproduce a tune whose words we once knew; they still exert an influence, although we do not pronounce them, and each group of sounds corresponding to a word forms a distinct whole, the tune being scanned much as a sentence might be. But words and phrases themselves result from social conventions that determine their meaning and function. The model of our analysis always comes from outside ourselves.

Moreover, we also recall tunes that are not songs, and songs whose words we have never heard. In these instances, the tune or song has been analyzed into rhythmic patterns. Strange as it may seem, one's merely tapping his finger on a table, reproducing the rhythm of a tune, may suffice to recall it for us. This is basically no different from recalling a song by means of its accompanying words. The taps, separated by intervals of varying length—whether short or rushed, regular or double time—have all the same sound. Nonetheless, they evoke a series of sounds of different pitch and intensity. But the same is true of words, which have no resemblance to the tunes they accompany. We will cease to be amazed by all this if we note that rhythm, like words, recalls to us not sounds but the manner in which we have analyzed their succession. Regarding this aspect, even in words themselves, rhythm may very well play the principal role. Singing from memory, don't we often retrieve the words as we recall the rhythm? We scan the verse, group the syllables two by two, and then, when we wish to speed up or slow down the song, change the rhythm.

If rhythm, in short, plays the major role here, then the whole problem turns on knowing what rhythm is. Does it not exist in nature? Could not an isolated man find by himself in sonorous space these rhythmic divisions? Rhythm need not be received from others if some natural phenomena could suggest it to him. But the sounds of nature alone do not follow any rhythmic pattern. Rhythm is the product of social life. The individual by himself could not invent it. Work songs, for example, arise from regular repetition of like motions among cooperating workers. Were these motions rhythmic in themselves, the songs would not provide the service expected of them. The song offers a model to the cooperating workers; the rhythm flows from the song into their movements. Hence it assumes a prior collective agreement. Our languages are rhythmic. Rhythm enables us to distinguish words and phrases that otherwise blend together, allowing no mental hold on the continuous and vague surface they form. At a very young age, we are familiarized with musical "beat." But society, not nature, has done this for us.

This society is composed mostly of people who are not knowledgeable in music. The popular tunes and songs they hear and repeat are as different from the sonatas or symphonies played by major orchestras as the layman's rhythm is different from the musician's measured time. Imagine that a musically uneducated person were to attend the performance of a difficult work. He would remember nothing of the piece, or at the most he would remember tunes to be sung—that is, those tunes most similar to ones with which he is familiar. Thus only a melody, a march or dance, may be extracted from a symphony or lyrical drama; those separate most easily and enter quite naturally into that framework of songs that the public understands, readily accepts, and remembers.

Why do we retain only this sequence of sounds and no other? We immediately grasped its simple rhythm and discovered in its movements a tempo, a balance, quite familiar from what we already know. Occasionally, a serious work gains favor with the public through its most commonplace and coarse qualities or, rather, through qualities that were never intended by the composer at its inception but became so when the public laid hands on it. Thus the "Ride of the Valkyries" became part of the repertoire of military music, and the "Waking of Springtime" is sung in the same tones and spirit as any old sentimental song. It is not Wagner's fault that a well-educated audience is no longer able, except with great effort, to view these pieces only as parts of a whole work. In the heyday of Italian opera, as Wagner himself points out, people attended primarily to hear certain rousing pieces of music designed to show off most favorably the vocal range of a tenor or prima donna. As for the rest of the opera, the music was no more than grace notes, the audience talking out loud and not even listening. Wagner wished, by contrast, to incorporate the vocal portions into the whole development of the music, so that the human voice would be only one among many instruments. He could not prevent the public, however, from removing from the totality of his works certain portions seemingly written as songs.

In the silence that reigns at the beginning of a concert, a space is defined from the first measure, into which no noise, not even a remembrance of noises, may penetrate from outside. Musician and audience forget the melodies and songs that ordinarily float in the memory. To understand the music now being heard is no longer a question of referring to these conventional models that society at large provides and keeps continually before us. Rather, the society of musicians unwinds before us a kind of invisible tape demarcated abstractly in a manner unrelated to any traditional or familiar rhythms. Let us examine this particular rhythm, which is different from that of language and not derived from it.

These abstract demarcations could not possibly serve to make the actual sequence of notes reappear in the memory of the musician or the person who knows and listens to the music. Measures in music merely represent so many identical intervals of time and are no more than empty frameworks. The sequence of sounds must be given on the score where the notes are written down or in the air through which the sounds travel to the musicians' audience. But we also must know how to reproduce or hear these sounds within the context of the measure. This cannot be accomplished by following with the eyes the baton of the conductor or by imparting to any part of his body a rhythmical movement. If performing, one must practice making the most frequent combinations of notes fit into a measure; if listening, one must be proficient at analyzing each sequence of notes for the demarcations by measures. But neither skill is natural, since this rhythm and this measure are not in themselves natural. The rhythm of musicians, in fact, has nothing in common with other rhythms. They correspond to acts not necessarily musical— i.e., marching, dancing, even speaking (which have as their principal purpose the communication of thought, not the reproduction of sounds). Musical rhythm presupposes, on the contrary, a purely sonorous space as well as a society of people concerned solely with sounds.

In a purely sonorous space, people having a very refined sense of hearing would identify many nuances, many relationships among the sounds, that would escape the average person. Since, from a musical viewpoint, one of the essential qualities of sound is duration, including the duration of the intervals separating one sound from another, these people would be sensitive to differences of time unnoticeable to the average person. Imagine that people thus talented and interested solely in sounds associate together to compose, perform, and hear musical works. Admission to such a group would require one to be able to apply very sensitive instruments of measurement to the pitch, tone, intensity, speed, and duration of any possible combination of sounds. Rhythm and measurement would be subject, in such a milieu, to much stricter rules than in an ordinary group where musical sensations are closely associated to other sensations. There is no room for objecting, moreover, that this difference between common rhythm and musician's rhythm is merely in degree and not in kind, because in both instances times and intervals are measured out. Wherever measurement becomes paramount, can there be any other difference than in the degree of precision required by and imposed on it? That is why the familiar rhythms of speech and movement are not enough for the musician. He seeks rhythm not outside sonorous phenomena but in the musical material itself, in sounds as they are perceived only by musicians. While this legitimate and very fruitful convention tends to close the gap with nature, since the laws of sound as formulated have a physical foundation, it remains a genuine convention all the same because it is oriented not solely to natural data as perceived by people who do not belong to the society of the musician.

Although thus permeated with convention, music often draws inspiration, it is true, from nature. Every type of sound produced by man or thing has passed into musical composition: the rustling of the wind among the leaves, the murmuring of water, the rumbling of thunder, the noises of an army on the march or a crowd in uproar, the varying accents of the human voice, and popular or exotic songs. But music transforms, in accordance with its own laws, what it borrows from human or natural milieus. Conceivably, if art thus imitates nature, it borrows some of nature's effects also. Certain works seem built on nonmusical themes, as though to reinforce interest in the music by the attraction of drama. The titles of such compositions suggest that the author wished to awaken in his listeners emotions of a poetic nature, to evoke various scenes and figures in their imagination. This tendency is probably due to the soceity of musicians not being able to restrain or to isolate itself from society in general. However, musicians are occasionally more exclusive, and it is among them that the feeling for what might be called "pure music" is found.

Let us consider the hypothetical situation of a musician remaining within the circle of musicians. What happens when he introduces a theme borrowed from nature or society into a sonata or symphony? First of all, if this theme has retained for him the character of its source, it has done so through its genuinely musical qualities. Whereas a layman is attracted by a passage in a sonata because it can be sung, a musician fixes his attention on a song in a village festival because it can be written out and then used as the theme for a sonata or orchestral composition. The layman separates the melody from the sonata; conversely, the musician separates the song from other songs, the tune from the words, and even a certain portion of the tune from the rest. Thus separated, pared down, impoverished of a portion of its substance, the tune is now transferred into the group of musicians to appear before long in a new form. Associated with other sequences of sounds and perhaps integrated into a whole piece, its value, the value of its parts, will be determined by its relationships with hitherto foreign musical elements. If it functions as theme, it is developed, however, in accordance with musical rules—that is, the musician will draw out what is certainly contained within it but what could be discovered only by a musician. If it functions as theme, it will give its particular coloring to each part of the piece in which it appears; likewise, it will itself undergo a transformation in each instance, but of a completely different kind than were it, for example, the refrain of a song that takes on a different meaning depending on the words of the couplet last sung. Thus this musical essence need not preserve an imprint, or invoke a remembrance or idea, of that from which it was extracted.

Since music thus sets off sounds from all other types of sensory data, we sometimes imagine that it separates us from the external world. Of course, sounds have a material reality. They are physical phenomena. But let us confine ourselves to auditory sensations, since the musician seldom concerns himself with anything else. If music comes from without, nothing forces us to take that external reality into account. Whereas colors, forms, and other material qualities are linked to objects, musical sounds are peculiar in being found only in relationship with other sounds. As nothing in nature resembles the works of musicians, we readily imagine that they escape the laws of the external world and exist solely through the power of the mind. The world into which music conveys us would therefore be the inner world.

Let us observe a little more closely. A combination or sequence of musical sounds may seem to us separated from any object only because it is itself an object. This object, it is true, exists only for the group of musicians. But what guarantees for us the existence of any fact, being, or quality, if not the agreement concerning it established by the members of a society—i.e., among those interested in it? A person does not simply draw from himself, and himself alone, a new theme, a combination of sounds that his mind has created from nothing. Rather, he discovers it in the world of sounds that the society of musicians alone is able to explore; it is because he accepts that society's conventions, and is even more permeated by them than the other members, that he achieves success. Musical language is not some instrument invented after the fact to fix and communicate to musicians what certain among them have spontaneously imagined. On the contrary, it is this language that has created music. Without it there would be no society of musicians, not even musicians, just as without laws there would be no city and no citizens. Far from isolating us in the contemplation of our inner states, music makes us come out of ourselves. It resituates us in a group that is far more exclusive, exacting, and disciplined than any other that may enclose us. But this is natural, for it involves precise data that allow no variation and require an apprehension and reproduction of the highest exactitude.

Schopenhauer, in criticizing Leibniz's definition of music as *"execitium arithmeticae occultum nescientis se numerare animi"* (literally, "an operation of occult arithmetic made by a mind ignorant of the fact it counts"), recognized its accuracy, but adds that it refers only to the crust, the dress, the externals, of the art of sound.[1] Similarly, it might be objected that I describe accurately the memory of the musician with regard to his technique, but that there is reason to distinguish between, on the one hand, remembrances of movements or symbols, even memories of sounds as they can be produced by these movements or represented by these symbols, and, on the other hand, the impression caused in us by these sounds, whether we are producing them or listening to them. Everything we have said would apply only to the first of these two aspects; it might even be granted that our memory is dependent on the society of musicians in anything presupposing the knowledge and practice of the rules of nusic. But musical feelings, and even the feelings awakened within us by music, are something else. These feelings would certainly be paramount in, if not the sum total of, a musician's remembrance of a performance, as performer or listener—in any case, such feelings may be disregarded only under penalty of reducing his playing or listening to a purely automatic activity.

When a musician resumes his place in the orchestra and finds before him a score that he has read many times, it could be said that nothing has changed, that the same notes will be reproduced in the

[1] Arthur Schopenhauer, *Die Welt als Wille und Vorstellung* (Leipzig: Reclam), p. 338.

same order and with the same tempo. We might add that his play-ing would be the same, to all intents and purposes, and that phono-graph recordings of the first and last performance might be difficult to distinguish. Now will it be said that we have here the same musi-cal remembrance? But such a remembrance includes, and only in-cludes, whatever is reducible in memory to a material mechanism, whatever can be fixed on paper or in the imprint or design, as is anything material and inert. But does memory comprise nothing else? Whether one is sight-reading or performing, it is not enough to understand the symbols: an artist interprets them in his own way, inspired either by his momentary or by his more permanent emotional disposition. He has his own characteristic temperament, so that an element of originality (of which he is aware) enters into his impressions, even his purely musical impressions, as it does into his playing. Why would he not evoke, on the occasion of this piece or that passage, his frame of mind during a previous playing or hearing, the nuances that must distinguish his musical sensations from those of any other person? Is it not by isolating himself from musicians, by forgetting that he is a member of the group and bound by their conventions, that he will retrieve the remembrance of these moments, instances when he has been in touch, in the pro-foundest depths of self, with a world that music has at that moment made accessible to him?

However, nothing proves that musical sensitivity, even in its ap-parently most personal nuances, isolates us from others and encloses us within ourselves. The society of musicians, though based on rules, is composed of human beings. It is a society of artists, as in-terested, perhaps even more so, in the musical talents of its mem-bers as in the techniques of its art. It is well aware that rules are no substitute for genius. It recalls, along with the musical works them-selves, those who have enriched them with new accents and tech-niques, who have deepened the substance of music either by regain-ing the inspiration of the author in these works or by penetrating more deeply into their meanings. Musicians observe one another, compare themselves, agree on fit subjects for admiration or enthusi-asm, on certain hierarchies. Music, too, has its gods, saints, and high priests.

The memory of the musician is filled, therefore, with data about human beings, but about those who have been connected with music. In my opinion, musical feeling does not grow in height or depth by ridding itself of technique and isolating itself from all that has occurred within the society of musicians. The temperament and talent of a musician are noted and recognized, valued and admired, because those interested in sounds find in the expression of his sensitivity an ever-present model that best realizes, most profoundly embodies, the tendencies of the group. He achieves greater stature through his musical genius, but it is as if he were possessed by an invisible demon, one whose spirit pervades every musician even though it allows itself to be captured and mastered only by a very few. Where is this genius to be found, if not in the midst of the group? Now everyone can see him, recognize him, and recognize himself in him.

Beethoven, struck deaf, nonetheless produced his most beautiful works. Is it sufficient to state that, living in his musical memories from that point on, he was enclosed within an inner universe? He was isolated only in appearance. Musical symbols, the sounds and combinations of sounds, remained with him in all their purity. He had not invented them, since they were the language of the group. In reality, he was more immersed than ever, and more than anyone else, in the society of musicians. He was never alone. And it was this world full of objects, more real to him than the real world, that he explored; in this world he discovered, for those who inhabited it, new territories that are nonetheless part of their domain, which they in turn immediately and rightfully have taken over.

Perhaps our conception of music is somewhat narrow. After all, it is not necessary to be familiar with the rules of this art, to be capable of reading and interpreting notes, to enjoy a concert. Suppose we ask a musician what he imagines, what he thinks about, when he listens to a symphonic theme unfolding. He may reply that he imagines nothing, that it is enough for him simply to listen, that he is perpetually in the present and any thought would distract him from what alone is important—namely, the music itself. A listener who follows the piece on a score may agree with him. But there are others who love to hear music because they can then, apparently, think more freely about some other topic of interest, work their imagination more actively, and be less distracted from their meditation or reverie. Stendhal states that "for me, the best music is that to which I can listen while thinking about what makes me happiest." Again, "my thermometer is this: when a piece of music projects me into the highest thought about the subject which occupies me, whatever it might be, that music is excellent to me. All music which causes me to think about music is mediocre for me."[2] Whether we are sad, joyful, loving, hopeful, or preoccupied with projects, whatever our mood, music seems at certain moments to sustain, deepen, and increase its intensity. It is as if the succession of sounds presents us with a kind of plastic material without definite meaning but ready to receive whatever our mind molds out of it.

How are we to account for this remarkable mental duality, the ear perceiving sounds and rhythm while the mind pursues some meditation or fantasy seemingly out of touch with reality? Is it because music turns our attention away from external objects and creates a void in our mind, so that any thought that pops up finds an open field? Furthermore, is it because musical impressions follow one another like a continuous and undammed current, suggesting the spectacle of a continually changing creation, so that our thoughts are swept away in this current and we have the illusion that we ourselves are creative, that nothing hinders our will and fantasy? This genuine feeling of free imaginative creation is better accounted for by the contrast between the milieu where we happen to be at the moment and the milieu in which our mind ordinarily carries on its activities.

The thought and sensitivity, I would assert, of the musician who is only a musician is obliged to pass occasionally along quite narrow paths and must remain within a definite zone. In effect, sounds obey a singularly precise body of laws. One can understand and feel the music of the musician only if one complies fully with these laws. By contrast, a person who attends a concert in order to enjoy in particular the pleasure of thinking and freely imagining need comply with the musical laws only to the point of feeling the change of mi-

[2] Stendhal, *Lettres à ses amis*, p. 63.

lieu, of being lulled and swept away by the rhythm. At least he then escapes those conventions that still weigh on him as a member of other groups and inhibit his thought and imagination. The contrast between these two kinds of groups is so great that, though he belongs to both, he feels the pressure of neither. He must maintain this equilibrium position. Were he to become too preoccupied in the music, to make an effort (often poorly rewarded) to understand it, he would lose that feeling of freedom, as he would were he, while in the concert, to forget insufficiently the tedium and cares of that group external to the society of musicians from which he came and which he wishes to leave behind. He might hear the same music that he had heard before, but it would no longer produce the same effect in him; comparing that remembrance with this present impression, he would exclaim, "Is that all there was to it?"

There would therefore be two ways of listening to music. Attention might focus on sounds and their combinations—that is, on purely musical objects and aspects. Or rhythm and the succession of notes might accompany our thoughts, as we become caught up in the flow of music.

This feeling of liberty, of broadening of mind, of creative power, which is intimately bound up with musical movement and sonorous rhythm, can certainly be described in general terms. But it arises only in listeners sensitive to the music itself. Of course, such listeners, besides being at least potential musicians, share with composers and performers a common humanity. Naturally, the vibrations that these sequences and combinations of sounds communicate to them are occasionally translated into human feelings and conceptions common to musical artists, other artists, and even to man as a whole whether appreciative or not of the art.

Let us read what Robert Schumann wrote on this subject, on "the difficult question of knowing how far instrumental music has the right to represent thoughts and events."[3]

One is certainly mistaken in believing that composers take up pen and paper with the wretched idea of expressing, describing, or paint-

[3] Robert Schumann, *Gesammelte Schriften Über Musik und Musiker* (Leipzig: Reclam I), pp. 108–109.

ing this or that object. But one ought not to underestimate contingent influences and external impressions. Often an idea works unconsciously alongside musical fantasy, the eye alongside musical fantasy, the eye alongside the ear. Indeed, as it works, musical fantasy retains in the tones and the sounds certain patterns which can condense and develop the music into definite forms as it unfolds. The more the thoughts or forms, evoked in us as we hear the sounds, contained musically visible elements, the more the expression of the composition will be poetic or plastic. . . . Why should Beethoven, in the midst of his fantasies, be surprised by the thought of immortality? Why shouldn't his memory of a great but fallen hero inspire in him a great work? Does music truly have nothing to tell us of Italy, the Alps, a view of the sea, a dawn in spring?[4]

Later on, he writes: "In the beginning music could only express simple mental states like joy (major key) or sorrow (minor key). Less cultured people can scarcely imagine that it is capable of translating the finer emotions; it is this that makes them uneasy before the intelligence of all the great masters such as Beethoven or Schubert." But he adds that "it is in penetrating more deeply into the mysteries of harmony that music has become capable of expressing the most delicate nuances of feeling." Is this "feeling" without qualification or feeling as it can be felt and expressed only by a musician? For, it must be repeated, musicians are also human beings. Although they can move from the technical level to the human level, what is essential is that they remain in the musical world. Once again, Schumann has provided us with a lucid statement. "A cultured musician will study a Madonna of Raphael as faithfully as a painter might a symphony of Mozart. Moreover, for a sculptor the whole actor becomes an immobile statue, for a painter a whole poem becomes a picture, and the musician transmutes the whole picture into sounds." Likewise, I would say that conceptions and feelings are transmuted into music: whether a person belongs to the musicians' circle or merely remembers once having been immersed

[4] This romantic conception is most clearly opposed by Edward Hanslick, *Vom Musikalisch-Schönen* (1857), for whom music can express and translate nothing but itself.

in it, how would he be able to evoke these conceptions and feelings later if not by reconstructing about himself, at least in thought, that very society with its techniques, conventions, and ways of judging and feeling?

Let us return to the consideration that was our point of departure. It concerned the function of signs in memory, as we have been able to illustrate with regard to music. Musicians need to evoke many remembrances in order to learn to perform or to sight-read music or merely to listen, recognize, and distinguish sounds, their value and intervals. Where are these remembrances found, and in what form are they conserved? As I stated, were a musician's brain to be examined, a number of mechanisms would be found, none of them set up spontaneously. Indeed, such mechanisms cannot be set up merely by isolating the musician before things, by letting natural noises and sounds act upon him. To explain such cerebral machinery, relationships must be established between corresponding (symmetrical or complementary) mechanisms functioning in other brains, in other men. Moreover, this correspondence is achieved only because a prior agreement has been established among these men: but such an agreement implies the conventional creation of a system of material symbols or signs having well-defined meaning.

These signs represent so many commands given by the society of musicians to its members. These signs are numerous, since there is a considerable quantity of sound combinations, which in turn form wholes with parts having well-defined positions in time. With sufficient practice, musicians can recall the elementary commands. But most cannot memorize the complex commands encompassing very extensive sequences of sounds. Hence they need to have before them sheets of paper on which all the signs in proper succession are materially fixed. A major portion of their remembrances are conserved in this form—that is, outside themselves in the society of those who, like themselves, are interested exclusively in music. Even the remembrances within them—remembrances of notes, signs, and rules—are found in their brain and mind only because they belong to this society, which has enabled their acquisition. These remem-

brances exist by dint of their relatiohship to the group of musicians; they are preserved only because individuals belong or once belonged to that society. Hence it can be said that the remembrances of musicians are conserved in a collective memory that extends through space and time as long as their society does.

Although emphasis has been on the function that signs play in the musical memory, we should remember that similar observations can be made for many other cases. Printed books, indeed, conserve remembrances of word, phrases, and series of phrases, just as scores fix remembrances of sounds and sequences of sounds. In the theater, actors have roles just as musicians have parts. They must learn them by heart with the help of scripts; even if the written words are not before their eyes, they have recently reread them, perhaps during preceding rehearsals. Moreover, a prompter is present—that is, a representative of the society of actors—who reads in their place and can instantly supplement the faltering memory. In both cases, but for different reasons, the objective of the society would not be attained were the words not literally repeated, if responses did not follow the questions, and if participants did not step in at the correct moment.

Furthermore, church and theater language is more conventional than ordinary language. It is, one might say, language to the second power, because it could not be invented by either an isolated individual or by an individual of society in general. Nobody talks in the street, even in the everyday world, like actors on a set or the faithful during prayers. Of course, expressions taken from various milieus may pass into the language of drama or comedy. Similarly, prayers of a different character—i.e., prayers for a special occasion, local prayers, prayers for a person—may be introduced into traditional texts and, for a moment, the congregation speaks the language of the nation, province, or family. But anything like this must assume a literary form (in the theater) or an edifying form (in the church), as if each had merely recovered something of its own once lost, instead of having borrowed from the general society new means of expression. In all these characteristics, the society of actors or of the faithful resembles the group of musicians and evinces a similar type of collective memory.

This resemblance probably holds true in part because of the important place music has in these types of gatherings (even if, in the present, there are neither chants in church nor musical instruments in the theater). Despite whatever reality and importance these analogies may have, there is quite a great difference between the society of musicians and any other community using signs and requiring its members to literally repeat the same words. When attending a play, why do we ask the actors to reproduce the printed text exactly? We do so because the author's text is well suited to his thought—that is, to the characters he wishes to portray, to the traits and emotions he wishes us to experience. Here speeches, words, sounds, are not their own end, but pathways to the meaning, to the feelings and ideas expressed, to the historical milieu or figures depicted—in short, to what is most important. This is what our thoughts fasten on to, and this is what we will evoke when we recall attending that play. But we will not have to retrieve the exact words heard. We have other means of conserving through memory the remembrance of what we then experienced. In other words, the collective memory of these gatherings in which plays are presented doubtless keeps the texts of works, but even more so what these words have evoked, which is no longer language or sounds. Similarly, the faithful seek to remember not so much the words of their prayers as the religious feelings they experienced. Again the words diminish in importance and, if their exact repetition is prized, it is because the spirit is thought inseparable from the letter. All the same, it is the spirit primarily that the collective memory of the religious group seeks to preserve.

Musicians, in contrast, stop with sounds and never search beyond. Satisfied with having created a musical atmosphere in which they have unfolded musical themes, they are interested in anything suggested by, but not expressible in, their language. It will always be easy and legitimate for the poet, philosopher, novelist, as well as the lover or the ambitious, to half forget the music being played at the performance they attend, and to isolate themselves in meditations or revery. Wholly different is the attitude of the musician, whether performing or listening. At such a moment, he is immersed in the milieu of those concerned solely with creating or listening to combinations of sounds—he is totally involved in that society. The others mentioned have only partially engaged themselves in this society, sufficient to isolate themselves from their usual milieu, from the group to which they adhere most closely and have, in fact, never really left. But then to guarantee the conservation and remembrance of musical works, no appeal can be made to images and ideas, as is the case with the theater. That is, no appeal can be to the meaning, because a sequence of sounds has no other meaning than itself. Perforce it must be retained as such, in full.

Music is, to tell the truth, the only art on which this condition is imposed, because it develops totally in time, because it is unconnected to anything stable and thus is recaptured only by constant re-creation. This is why there is no example in which one perceives more clearly that the possibility of retaining a mass of remembrances with every nuance and in precise detail requires bringing into play every resource of the collective memory.